ACCELERATE

The Ultimate Guide for FRANCHISEES to Maximize Local Marketing and Boost Sales

Ford Saeks

This book is perfect for single and multi-unit franchise owners, management, and staff. It's designed to be compliant and used in conjunction with YOUR franchise brand's systems and guidelines. It's applicable for all franchise revenue models, including B2B, B2C, retail, and services brands. The concepts, strategies, and tactics can be used successfully with any franchise business or industry selling products and services through a franchise system.

Saeks, Ford, 1961 –

ACCELERATE The Ultimate Guide for FRANCHISEES to Maximize Local Marketing and Boost Sales by Ford Saeks

Paperback: ISBN: 978-1-884667-40-4

Hardcover: ISBN: 978-1-884667-46-6

Kindle / EPUB: ISBN: 978-1-884667-41-1

LCCN - 2020924578

1. Business Franchises 2. Marketing 3. Selling

Printed in the United States of America

Publisher: Prime Concepts Group Press publishes in a variety of print and electronic formats and by print-on-demand. Some material included with standard print versions of this book may not be included in e-books, audio, or in print-on-demand. PrimeConcepts.com

Special thanks to Aliesa George, Devan Horning, Randy Gage, Michelle Datin and Sheryl Green, and the team at Prime Concepts Press for helping me give birth to this book. Cover design credit goes to Jenna Giberson and Devan Horning

For **volume book purchases**, media interviews, or book signings, please contact Profit Rich Results at ProfitRichResults.com or call 1-316-844-0235.

For **Franchise Keynote Presentations & Training** visit FranchiseTrainingSolutions.com.

A great companion book to this one is Ford's ***SUPERPOWER! A Superhero's Guide to Leadership, Business, and Life***. Get your copy today at www.SuperpowerBook.com or on Amazon or your favorite book retailer.

What People Are Saying...

"Ford Saeks is an international expert on all matters of marketing and branding. In this book, he shares solid ideas and practical strategies to build your business and enhance your life."

— Dr. Nido R. Qubein, Executive Chairman
Great Harvest Bread Co.

"As the largest multi-unit owner of Edible Arrangements® Franchises, I have learned firsthand the importance of effective local marketing in driving business success. That's why I highly recommend Ford's new book, *ACCELERATE*, to any franchise owner looking to increase their reach and impact in their local community. It's a practical and valuable resource that has already made a significant impact on my family of franchises."

— Uri Geva. Largest Multi-unit Franchisee
Edible Arrangements®

"Many factors go into franchise success, with developing a positive mindset being the foundation, following our systems, and executing with local area marketing. This book has helped fill the gap for our family of franchises. Thanks, Ford!"

— Becky Bongiovanni, Brand President
CarePatrol™ Franchise Systems, LLC

"I've got over a decade of experience as a franchise owner, and I'm always looking for ways to grow even faster. I love how practical *ACCELERATE* is for my team to help us spark ways to execute successfully, boost our local presence, and generate leads for my WOW 1 Day Painting Franchise. Thanks, Ford!"

— Craig Merrills, Franchise Partner
Wow 1 Day Painting

1

"As someone who knows the franchise industry, I can say that Ford Saeks KNOWS FRANCHISING. Ford is a great resource and has helped me with my digital presence and marketing too. He's generous and smart, and a nice guy on top of it all!"

— John Francis, CEO
Next Level Franchise, Inc.

"We picked Ford Saeks out of a very elite group of keynote speakers. Our owners come from a very diverse group both geographically and all walks of life, and the interaction was phenomenal. The way he laid out the topics and cultivated exchange is the best that we've seen in any national meeting to date."

— Michael Brickner, President
Precision Door Service (A Neighborly Company)

"Ford Saeks really delivered! He was very engaging and got our franchisees thinking and left them with tangible things they can use to grow their business."

— Betsy Hamm, CEO
Duck Donuts

"We really enjoyed your Business Growth keynote presentation. It was standing room only, you packed it out! I left with tons of ideas and concepts that our franchisees can implement immediately."

— Kim Hanson, CEO
LearningRx Franchise Corporation

"Our franchisees absolutely LOVED him! His material was 'spot-on' for what we wanted delivered and his actionable takeaways truly resonated with our team."

— Madison Halman, Director of Training
Liberty Tax Service

"Having booked Ford for multiple franchise events over the years, our franchise brands love his keynote presentations and books because they're relevant to new franchisees, multi-unit owners, and producers looking for ways to grow their businesses."

— Katrina Mitchell, Chief Match Maker
Franchise Speakers

"This amazing book is loaded with practical, proven strategies that you can use immediately to get what you want in every area of your life."

— Brian Tracy, CEO
Brian Tracy International Inc.

"Ford has been one of the best keynote speakers that we've ever brought in to help our franchise owners learn about accelerating their business, driving more revenue, and increasing profitability. He inspired our team and more importantly gave us actionable items we can take back and implement in our businesses to set us up for success."

— Brandon Moxam, Vice President
US Lawns

"When it comes to marketing, Ford Saeks is the real deal. This book is filled with practical insights that can be applied to any business wanting to dominate with local marketing. He tells it like it is, without the fluff, in easy-to-consume and implement language. Get a copy for everyone on your team."

— Shawn Engbrecht, CEO
CASS Global Security

"We hired Ford Saeks to do a marketing consulting project for our franchise company, and we liked it so much we hired him to do a second one specifically on franchise sales. The bottom line is that I liked him so much as a keynote speaker that we became a client, twice!"

— Roger J. Murphy, CEO & Founder
Murphy Business Sales

Dedication

For Zors and Zees…

I dedicate this book to those franchisors (Zors) that risk their time, energy, and money to turn their ideas into successful franchise brands. And to those franchisees (Zees) that become part of their brand's family of owners, bringing valuable products and services to local communities. You have my respect and admiration.

ACCELERATE

Table of Contents

Achieving the Franchise Breakthrough...

Introduction

No matter where you're at right now with the success of your business, there is always some improvement, growth, or expansion you'd like to see. And right now, wherever you're sitting, and in every situation, there is a GAP... And you're not there yet, and no matter what, people always feel that that GAP is truly unique to them.

The interesting thing is that in all my research, consulting experiences, and keynote presentations working with franchisees throughout the world, small and large, from start-ups to billion-dollar brands, B2B and B2C, when I'm working with a business owner or staff like any of you reading this book, I have found that GAP always comes down to one of three problem areas:

- **Mindset**

- **Strategies**

- **Tactics**

Before we break those down, allow me to take a moment to congratulate you. Buying and growing your franchise (whether it's your 1st or your 100th) is exciting! You're part of a fantastic industry and business model that offers so many unique benefits.

Over the past couple of years, many business owners (including me!) have had to reexamine how we do business. What may have worked in the past, simply isn't as effective anymore. We've all had to adapt to operate in a changing world, and this journey has been challenging for many. As I'm sure you've already discovered...

It's not what you know... it's how well you execute!

I know what you're facing day-to-day; I'm with you. Finding staff and retaining top talent is challenging. Profit margins are being squeezed through increased costs and supply-chain disruptions. Generational differences in the workforce cause communication and engagement issues. The way that people make buying decisions has changed. There are government, economic, and technology disruptions, and that's just to name a few of the internal and external obstacles facing you on your journey.

ACCELERATE is designed to help you reignite your passion, people, and processes in alignment with your brand's standards, to help you elevate your local brand awareness, and increase sustainable sales. Let me share a little more about who I am and why I'm uniquely qualified to write this book.

Helping businesses add value and make a profit is what makes me throw the sheets off and jump out of bed each morning. Plain and simple. I've spent a lifetime doing what I love: starting, building, growing, and selling businesses, inventing products, and helping others bring their ideas to fruition.

I came from next to nothing. I was kicked around in the foster care system, lived in the housing projects of North Minneapolis, and was on a work release program for troubled youths through junior and senior high school. I've been in the trenches just like many of you, responsible for every aspect of my business. I've made more mistakes in business than I can count, with each lesson helping me refine what works and what doesn't. I've hired wrong, kept employees too long that should have been freed up for new opportunities (aka fired). I became complacent at times, resting on my laurels of past success. I've diversified, only to find out that I deworsified.

I've listened to so-called experts, only to find out they were teaching theory and didn't have the practical, real-world experience that was applicable to me and my business. I've grown too fast, too slowly, too big, and have been under-capitalized too many times, having to bootstrap cash just to make payroll. I've had vital employees I've invested years developing leave to go to the competition or start competing directly with me in the same markets. I've had accounting staff embezzle hundreds of thousands and dealt with petty theft of inventory losses.

Since I opened my very first company when I was only 15, I've owned service-based businesses (carpet cleaning, painting, and home improvement services) and product-based businesses (manufacturing a line of sporting goods, distributing children's products, and built a dealer network of medical safety products sold to hospitals and labs).

My sporting goods business employed over 120 people, and we sold through multiple distribution channels including retail, direct, wholesale, chain stores, mass merchants like Walmart®, Sam's Club®, and Costco, a network of manufacturing reps, distributors, multiple export firms, through OEM methods (private labeling), and sold through specialty catalogs including SkyMall, Williams Sonoma®, and Sharper Image, just to name a few.

After I proved my success in business, I became known for taking ideas from a napkin to the marketplace and people began asking for help with their enterprises. I had both start-ups and existing companies coming to me for help. The new companies wanted to know how to get started and accelerate their learning curve, strategically plan, and launch new product lines. The existing companies wanted to expand their market share, gain a competitive edge, improve their reach and conversions, shorten the sales cycle, improve engagement, elevate the customer experience, accelerate their sales, and grow profitability.

Three key areas of focus in business are marketing and sales, business operations, and financial management

Business owners are typically only good at one of these areas (maybe two). After enough people came to me for help in these different areas, I realized that I needed to charge for my insights and guidance. So, I started the journey as a business growth consultant. Since then, I've helped thousands of businesses, many of which have been top franchise brands and their franchisees.

I've been hired to present at their annual company conferences, industry association meetings, and provide virtual and on-site training workshops too. As a franchise consultant and CEO of Franchise Training Solutions, we've also designed customized training and course curriculum in a variety of formats.

Now, I'm not just an expert because of my experience, but because of the collective experience of the many clients in a wide variety of market verticals that I've had the honor to work closely with over the years.

Whether you're struggling with your franchise business or just looking for guidance to do even better, you're in the right place and you're in good hands. Now is the perfect time to evaluate your local area marketing efforts, to stop doing the things that aren't working, keep doing the things that are, and start doing what you've never done before to achieve results you've never achieved.

There's Hope for Us

We all get bogged down, and we have days where we feel like it all gets lost, but today won't be one of those because this book will equip you with insights and many ways to accelerate your growth in any economic condition. Let's begin with the three keys we discussed at the start: Mindset, Strategies, and Tactics.

FIRST, either you don't have the right growth MINDSET, and you're struggling with negative self-talk or lacking positive focus. Or maybe you do have the right mindset. You're driven, you're so dialed in, but the SECOND component is the STRATEGY you have in place is not effective because your brand's franchise systems aren't being followed, and that's what's holding you back.

So, you could be working all day, and you have the right mindset, but without the strategy implementation, it's not yielding the results you want. A considerable advantage for you is that your franchise brand has provided you with the strategy, branded systems, resources, and best practices, but you still have to execute.

Or THIRD, it's related to the specific execution of the local TACTICS you're using or not using. For you, it might be your mindset, for some, it might be the strategies, and for others, it's executing tactics or a combination of these.

So, your goal as you read this book is to identify which of these areas of focus most resonate with you and capture the action steps related to how to maximize them. It's about being honest with yourself about where you are now, where you want to go, and what's holding you back, and then taking action in one of these areas.

And for some of you, it might be all three challenge areas, but I want you to start with one. Most importantly, I'm going to help you find your focus and demystify how to bridge that GAP. I promise you'll discover key distinctions and doable actions you can implement immediately.

Throughout this book, we're going to go through those three areas, the mindset, the strategies, and the tactics that you need to leverage to scale your business.

"Hey Ford, I've been in the franchise business for years, and I'm doing great. Am I wasting my time reading this book?"

Absolutely not. The strategies, tactics, and advice in this book will help you and your team improve your local area marketing and sales performance no matter which camp you fall into. Maybe you're a new franchise owner who just purchased your business and are now experiencing the "Now what?" phase, or perhaps you've been a successful "multi-unit" top-producer for years. You can use this book to reignite, reframe, and refocus. **Remember, it's not what you know... it's how well you execute!**

Let's dive a bit more into these two possible scenarios.

Scenario One: You're a New Franchise Owner

This past year, Joe purchased his first franchise. For years now, he's dreamed of being a business owner. From his first job in high school, flipping burgers at the local fast-food joint, Joe wanted to be his own boss. He did his research and investigated building his own business from scratch. Sure, he could do it. It would take a lot of hard work, start-up capital, and building his own brand recognition, but he could do it.

And then Joe learned about franchising. He knew that there were established companies that would give him the brand recognition, the blueprint, and the support he needed to be a successful business owner. He was in.

A few months later, Joe signed all the paperwork, invested his money, went through the brand's university training, hired his staff, and opened his doors. He held a ribbon-cutting, and all his family and friends came out to support him. It was one of the most exciting days of his life.

But where were the customers?

The doors had now been open for six months, and while a few customers trickled in each day, Joe was getting more and more concerned. Bills were due, employees had to be paid, and Joe was working 14-hour days, 7 days a week. Yet no matter how much time he spent in his business, he couldn't seem to get ahead and work on his business. He felt like he was treading water. His relationship with his wife was becoming strained. He started missing out on his kids' events.

This was not what Joe signed up for.

He began to get frustrated with himself and with the franchise opportunity he'd bought into. Why weren't they helping him? What were they doing to get customers in his door?

But enough about Joe.

Does this sound familiar? Can you relate to Joe's situation?

If you've recently purchased your first franchise, you were probably so excited in the beginning. You couldn't wait to open your franchise for business and serve thousands of happy customers with your products and services.

But... maybe you're still waiting for that growth you've dreamed of, or the freedom and the lifestyle that comes from being a successful franchise owner and entrepreneur. You're feeling stressed, frustrated, and unsure of how to turn your business around. Your family and friends are supportive, but they don't really understand what you're going through.

Or let's take a look at the other side of the coin...

Scenario Two: You're a Grizzled Veteran Franchise Owner

Michelle has owned multiple Quick Service Restaurant (QSR) locations for many years. She's followed the systems her franchisor put in place, is active on the franchise advisory committee, and attends the regional and national training events. She's reaping the rewards of her efforts, takes massive action following the brand standards, and is focused on local area marketing and sales activities to help her grow her business.

Of course, like any successful business owner, she's busy. Too busy. She's overseeing multiple locations, wearing multiple hats, and as happy as she is with the employees she's hired to manage her stores, she'd like to entrust them with more responsibility and take an even more hands-off approach to her business.

Does this hit close to home?

Maybe you've experienced the joys of franchise success, you follow your franchise brand's best practices, and you are growing in market share and locations. You've reached the point where you want to equip your leadership and marketing team, large or small, with a resource that you can use to help guide them to local marketing domination — all while staying in alignment with your franchise brand.

Don't worry. You've picked up the right book. You and your team can use this book to find, attract, and keep your customers, regardless of if your franchise model is Business-to-Business (B2B) or Business-to-Consumer (B2C).

For the sake of clarity, especially if you're new to franchising, it's essential to know the difference between these three terms.

Franchise: (BRAND) A business model in which a company (the franchisor) licenses its brand, products, and business systems to an independent business owner (the franchisee) in exchange for a fee. The franchisee agrees to follow the franchisor's established business model and operating procedures in order to operate the business. The franchisee pays the franchisor a percentage of their sales as a royalty fee, which helps to cover the costs of providing ongoing support and training to the franchisee.

Franchisor: (ZOR) A branded company that owns a successful business model and allows other businesses (franchisees) to use its brand, products, and business systems in exchange for a fee. The franchisor provides ongoing support and training to the franchisees to help them operate the business successfully.

Franchisee: (ZEE) An independent business owner/owner-operator who operates a business using the brand, products, and business systems of a franchisor in exchange for a fee. The franchisee is responsible for running the day-to-day operations of the business, including managing employees, marketing the business, and maintaining the premises.

A franchise can be a great way for a novice entrepreneur, investor, or seasoned business professional to get started because they can follow a successful business blueprint. When you buy a franchise and become a franchisee (owner), you are instantly part of a recognizable brand that already has operational systems, branded promotional materials, and some type of area or national advertising support.

I love the franchise model because the franchisor has already tested and proven what works and what doesn't. Just having a blueprint doesn't guarantee your success — you still have to follow their systems, claim top-of-mind awareness in your local territory through effective marketing and sales efforts, provide quality service experiences, and manage your operations and finances.

You are not alone on this journey.

This book is a powerful supplement to any franchise brand and business model. It's designed to read cover-to-cover or jump to the section that will help you address your top challenges.

You'll discover why it's essential to follow your brand's systems and best practices. It will help you to rethink, refocus, and reignite your passion for what you already know, while providing battle-tested local area marketing (LAM) and sales strategies and tactics designed to accelerate your business growth.

A FEW MORE THINGS... AND THEY'RE IMPORTANT.

My style is direct and straightforward.

I'm pretty sure that you'll come to appreciate my style. After all, you're not reading this book as a lazy Sunday read. If you want to be entertained and escape from your life, go grab a mystery novel. You're reading this book because you probably haven't had a free Sunday since you signed those papers and became a franchise owner. You're reading this book because you want to keep your momentum going, dominate your local marketing territory, and generate more revenue.

While I appreciate the use of acronyms and abbreviations, I may break the traditional grammar rules by using LAM, Local Area Marketing, marketing, and local marketing interchangeably to improve readability and consumption. Some brands use a Local Store Marketing Guide (LSM), others call it a marketing checklist or sales playbook.

What's clear with all brands is they want to drive traffic, generate leads, engage their team, implement consistently with their local marketing efforts, and accelerate revenue growth.

Please don't get distracted if you find spelling or grammatical errors, I've placed them intentionally to see if you're paying attention. Okay, seriously, if you do find them, please send me an email at fordspeaks@profitrichresults.com, and we'll update the print-on-demand files to continually improve this book. Plus, I'll reward you with special prizes.

Adapt, don't adopt.

I'm okay if you disagree with me, but these insights and tactics have been battle tested across the nation in my own ventures and with thousands of successful franchisees. Please note: It's essential that you adapt these insights and action steps for your brand's business model, territory, and stage of your business growth.

To adhere to your brand's standards, check for the appropriate approvals with new marketing methods to ensure you're operating within the established policies and accepted best practices.

Getting you to think and take action is the goal.

While writing this book, I've added context for those readers that may be at the emerging stage of their franchise business journey and those readers that are already very seasoned and successful. I guarantee you'll find insights and essential distinctions you can apply to help you accelerate your franchise business success.

Okay, let's GO!

Ford Saeks

Business Growth Accelerator

ACCELERATE Companion Study Guide and Tool Kit

Get instant access to the downloadable study guide, bonus how-to videos, templates, checklists, and more.

www.FranchiseTrainingSolutions.com/accelerate-tool-kit

PART I — MASTERING THE MARKETING MINDSET

Chapter 1: The Number One Essential for Growth…

At age 15 while sitting in my cell in the Hennepin County Detention Center, one of the counselor's intervened. He gave me a Sony Walkman audio player with *The Strangest Secret* by Earl Nightingale on cassette tape.

It was my first time hearing positive messaging and encouragement. It was exactly what I'd been missing in my youth. Up to that time, I was repeatedly told how stupid I was, that I was never going to amount to anything, and would most likely be dead before I reached 25.

I began thinking differently, focusing on the future possibilities rather than on the past and my problems. I started asking myself better questions, "How can I provide value, solve problems, and get paid for it?"

It was the beginning of my journey from victimhood to become victorious. And what led me to writing this book for you and the thousands of other people just like you. While maybe we haven't met in person yet, I want you to know that I believe in you and your continued success. Let's go back to that cell and see where the story went next…

I was getting released soon and wanted to earn money differently than how everyone in my neighborhood was earning money. That's a story for another time. My part-time job at Milts Supermarket bagging groceries and stocking shelves wasn't going to cut it. I was working for minimum wage, and in 1975 that was $2.10 an hour. I was motivated to make changes but had no marketable skills, or at least that's what I thought at the time. I was very street-smart and skilled at taking care of myself having moved out on my own at 12 years old. Looking back, I was really just a punk kid, disruptive, dysfunctional, and somewhat delusional. So, what business could I start? I didn't have any savings, credit cards, or mentors. What experiences could I turn into a profitable business?

Well, during my time at the detention center, the punishment for dropping "f-bombs" or fighting was to paint rooms in the building. And let me tell you, I became a f*cking good little painter. That's it. I'll start a painting business. The dream was born.

I went to my friends in school shop class and said, "Hey, can you design and print some flyers that say *Saeks Painting and Light Construction* with my phone number?" They were simple, but effective.

Armed with stacks of flyers, I hung them on bulletin boards, car windshields, and went door-to-door canvasing nice neighborhoods. After a couple of weeks, my first prospect call came in on my Radio-Shack reel-to-reel answering machine.

I was super excited, but what was I going to say to the prospect, how would I quote the job, what equipment and labor would be needed? I called the prospect, we'll call him Bob, and schedule the meeting for later that afternoon.

Excitement quickly turned to panic. I needed help. I didn't even own a paintbrush, how was I going to start a painting business? My negative self-talk threatened to derail my future plans, but those positive messages from *The Strangest Secret* kicked in, and I kept moving forward. I went to the Bryant Painting Supply store for help. I walked up to the counter and asked the manager, "Hey, I just started a new painting business, can you help me?"

After a bit of awkward dialogue and convincing him I'd buy all of my supplies from them if he'd help me, he smiled. "Yes, I can help you."

Fifteen minutes later, I walked out of the store with paint splattered on my clothing, a clipboard, calculator, and written instructions to help quote the job. I was in business. Well, sort of.

I arrived at Bob (the prospect's) house and knocked on the door. After going room to room and capturing all the measurements and getting a feel for the job (Did you know there were oil-based paints, flat based paints, KILZ®, etc.? I certainly didn't.) I used my most adult voice to say, "I have to go back to my office to prepare the proposal." Picture "hand gestured air quotes" here.

Of course, "my office" meant going back to the paint store for more help and to prepare the proposal. When I returned to Bob's house to deliver the written proposal for the painting job, his wife was now with him.

Keep in mind, I was only 15 years old. No experience with sales other than selling popcorn door-to-door as a fundraiser for Boys & Girls Clubs of America. This was decades before I learned the concept of crafting compelling marketing messages, sales tactics, and understanding different personality styles. Way before I discovered you need to preempt sales objections and modify the message to influencers vs decision makers, and tailor the sales narratives to females because they make many of the buying decisions for residential services.

With a big smile, I said, "Here's the proposal to paint the interior rooms in your house. The price is $1,025, and I'll need 50 percent up front and 50 percent upon completion of the job." (How else was I supposed to buy the supplies?) The wife eyed the proposal, eyed me up and down and said, "Do you have any experience?"

Ouch. Mayday, Mayday... Houston we have a problem. Actually, my inner dialogue was more like holy crap, what am I going to say now?

This was a critical point in my new business, which was only two hours old. Do I tell them that I repainted the whole north wing of the Hennepin County Detention Center? They might've still hired me. Or, they might've decided against having an inexperienced painter/juvenile delinquent in their house.

Being quick on my feet, I said, "If you're not 100 percent satisfied with the job, you don't have to pay."

The wife handed her husband a pen. "Honey, write him a check." I sat in my 1966 Chevelle with no tags or car insurance and stared at the deposit check. "I'm going to figure out how to do this," I said. I earned $35,000 in sales in my first year of business. In today's economy equivalence, that's about $200,000. Not too bad for first-year sales for a kid from the projects. Little did I know it then, but I had discovered the most important element of business for the franchise industry:

Local Area Marketing (LAM)

Top 12 Benefits of Local Area Marketing:

1. Helps you improve your visibility to attract new and repeat business.

2. Creates momentum and market penetration because you're more findable.

3. Increases lead generation through traditional and digital promotions.

4. Enhances brand loyalty and referrals because customers love buying local.

5. Creates new opportunities to develop beneficial connections with other nearby companies for potential future promotions.

6. Allows you to show up higher in search engines, especially on mobile devices.

7. You can take advantage of Google service listings that cater to local businesses.

8. Allows for geocoding of advertising.

9. Naturally increases your lifetime value (LTV) of customers.

10. Lowers your cost to acquire a customer and shortens the sales cycle.

11. Helps you attract staff and lower recruiting costs.

12. Gives you a competitive edge and accelerates business growth.

Local Area Marketing (LAM) is More Crucial Than Ever Right Now

During Covid, many businesses experienced a significant amount of growth. Take home services brands for example. People were home looking around and realizing they wanted to invest there.

They had stimulus checks to be able to fund it. I personally hired services for home cleaning, painting, landscaping, and more honey-do projects. While some brands were forced to modify or close, many other franchisees experienced a massive influx of demand.

Back in early 2022, that bump in demand started to naturally wane. Inflation, high loan rates, and other well-known macroeconomic concerns are all contributing to a slight decline in organic demand. The issue here is that many were so busy facilitating and serving their customers, that they reduced or even stopped investing in local area marketing. And by way of context, even before the pandemic, many brands I work with have shared how challenging it can be to get their owner-operators to invest in local area marketing.

Local Area Marketing is an Investment, Not an Expense

Finding ways to save money while increasing visibility is an ongoing challenge. That's why local area marketing should be seen as an investment rather than an expense. Local area marketing generates increased brand recognition to your local community, drives sales leads, improves customer loyalty, generates a referral culture, and when executed effectively, produces a tangible return-on-investment (ROI) — all of which are essential for growing your franchise in today's competitive landscape.

The good news is that this book is jammed full of LAM strategies and tactics. Combine them with the resources provided by your franchise home office, and you'll be set up for longevity and higher profits.

Sales Momentum When Demand is High

If your franchise is seasonal, demand will rise during your peak season. You may experience a backlog of business or capacity to serve that business. Naturally you may feel it's a good idea to reduce your local marketing spending because there will be more customers than you can accommodate. Maybe you quit running that half-page ad in a particular publication or cut back on digital marketing or reduced your pay-per-click advertising budget that produced a lot of leads. You cut expenses for the next three or four or five weeks, but suddenly leads come to a screeching halt and momentum stops.

I recognize that if you're booked out several weeks in advance, it may be prudent to reduce some of your efforts, but please do so with extreme caution. When you reduce your local marketing efforts, you reduce top-of-mind awareness, and you leave opportunities for your competition to gain market share. Worse, then it's even harder and more expensive to get momentum going again.

Double-down When Demand is Low

When you experience a downturn in revenue or sales, you may reduce or stop local marketing costs, thinking you're balancing the numbers. While that may look good on paper, it's not good in practice, and it stunts your growth or worse, can lead to bankruptcy. When sales are down, that's the time to overinvest in your local area marketing efforts to jumpstart demand and generate leads.

National Advertising is National Advertising

It's no longer possible (and never was a sustainable solution) to rely on just organic demand or the efforts the corporate brand office puts into national advertising efforts. It is not a good idea to rely solely on national advertising because you are the one with actual, in-person experience in your local markets. National advertising is national advertising and designed to help elevate brand awareness.

National Advertising shouldn't be the source of all your leads. Full stop.

Chapter 2: Common Obstacles We All Face

A multi-unit franchise owner called me a few months into the pandemic. He owned and operated several Quick Service Restaurants (QSRs), and he was having difficulty with his customers and staff.

Because of all the necessary safety protocols, the restaurant's focus shifted from providing excellent customer service to keeping everyone safe. Noble as this was, customers were getting annoyed at the lack of customer service displayed by the staff.

But that was just one problem.

The other challenge this franchise owner faced was staffing and turnover. It was becoming harder to attract, train, and retain staff at all levels. Recruiting was expensive. Many entry-level staff didn't seem to have a positive work ethic.

When he asked them why, they said, "Go ahead and fire me. I'll go across the street to your competition because they're hiring too." He was getting disheartened with the whole process and didn't know how to keep his employees happy enough that they'd stay.

When I work with franchise owners, I hear a lot of similar issues, no matter what brand, company, or industry they're in. The pandemic of 2020 brought its own set of challenges as businesses around the world learned the importance of adaptation. Now's the time (no matter when you're reading this book) to stop looking backward and look to the future. The past is gone, so let it go!

Common Obstacles to Growth

Let's look at a few common problems franchise owners believe stand in their way and see if you're experiencing the same issues. Don't worry; we'll get to the insights, strategies, and specific tactics to overcome these challenges and how to accelerate your business growth in future chapters.

Staffing Challenges Across the Board

Oh yeah. Chances are that you're working with an unskilled or under-skilled workforce and experiencing higher than desired turnover rates.

Are you making battlefield promotions, putting people in positions beyond their skill level just because they're a warm body and the last person standing?

Papa Murphy's franchisees staffing challenges. Their Bake-at-Home pizzas have been flying off the proverbial shelves, but with the government offering so much assistance and higher than regular unemployment payments, it was difficult to find anyone who wanted to work for minimum wage... let alone anyone good.

Many of the franchise brands I work with say their biggest challenge is finding, retaining, and engaging quality staff. But it isn't just saying "people don't want to work," there is more to it than that. To attract and maintain talent you will have to pay more up front now. Everything is more expensive, and people are expecting more in return for their time. From entry level to management level, you must be competitive in pay. That means you might be paying a first-time worker well more than your local minimum wage. Some operators don't understand that even though we sell products or services, we are still a people business. How much business is lost because you're understaffed?

We all need to develop our people and teams. Sounds simple right? Expectations with increased pay cause issues. Previously you could find external talent at a management level with the specific desired skill sets, but now that's not the case in many circumstances. You must find people you can teach and hopefully they're coachable.

Retention

Everyone is trying to attract talent. Some throw higher wages at people, some have benefits and perks you can't or don't offer, some maintain their buildings or vehicles better (who wants to work in a dump), and some just plain create a better environment through recognition and relationships.

People are stressed out

Period. The past few years we've had a pandemic, natural disasters, school shootings, inflation, recession, and everyone telling us what to be upset about. How you manage people and the relationships with them is important.

Maybe you have attracted top talent and may struggle to create the positive culture, leadership, and incentives to encourage them to stay with you. Developing a healthy workplace culture is essential for growth. Turnover costs continue to rise and effect all areas of our businesses. Yours and mine.

Buyer behaviors have changed

This is very true, and the influx of technology is leading the charge. Today, people leave home with three things: a wallet/purse, car keys, and a cell phone.

Twenty years ago, you'd never see someone standing in the aisles of a store, checking the price on Amazon or reviews on Google. Yelp didn't exist, and it certainly wasn't the first stop for a hungry potential customer.

However, times have changed, and customers have a world full of knowledge and choices at their fingertips. With "quarantine" becoming a household word, many buyers looked to the online space to fulfill just about all of their needs (and continue to do so). We'll discuss how you can use this to your advantage.

Increased competition

Yes. More choices and companies are offering similar or alternative solutions. You'd be hard-pressed to find someone with a completely unique product or service who didn't have to contend with an oversaturated local marketplace. This book will share several ways to leverage the difference between *finding new customers* and *being found*.

Generational differences

Absolutely! There are more generations in the workforce and the buying world than ever before and the only thing they have in common... is that they have very little in common. So don't get seduced by labels like Gen Z, iGen, Gen C, Gen X & Y, Millennials, and Boomers.

Love or hate them, the employment culture and buying processes have been disrupted as we knew it just a few years ago. To succeed, we must adapt how we communicate, enhance our workplace culture, and conquer the local marketplace.

We can't sell and market the way we used to

Forced to close storefronts and offices, many franchises could not operate as usual during the pandemic. For example, CarePatrol™, a senior care placement agency franchise brand, got all of its business from hospital and doctor referrals.

Unable to meet face-to-face, they were forced to compete in an online space with 100s of similar companies. As a result, their old competitive advantage went out the window, and as they adapted to the new normal, they were able to grow exponentially. We'll discuss in a future chapter how they overcame this situation.

Culture of mistrust

This isn't a political book, but no matter what side of the political fence you're on, there's a good chance that you may not trust government rhetoric, the mainstream media, or social media narratives. Consumers have lost faith in almost everything these days, and businesses are feeling the effects.

One of the benefits of buying into a franchise is having an established, time-tested brand behind you. A small mom-and-pop shop without a national brand name doesn't carry the same clout with consumers. Throughout this book, you'll discover how to build and develop that trust throughout your local marketing and sales efforts.

There's so much to do, and I don't have time

Many franchisees feel overwhelmed by the sheer nature of the demands of running a successful franchise. Operational demands, production and delivery of products and services, accounting and finance, cash-flow management, marketing and sales, and the list goes on.

While the focus of this book is local area marketing and increasing sales, I'll also be sharing several ways to get several hours back each week, improving your mindset and execution, leading to better enjoyment and quality of life. We'll dig deeper into this topic and helpful solutions to reclaim your time in an upcoming chapter.

Technological Disruptions

With technology changing at breakneck speeds, you need to have your head mounted on a swivel with at least one eye on future trends that may shape the way people interact, engage, communicate, and make purchases.

Just look at this list and think about the ways these advances have and will impact your personal and professional lives:

- Artificial Intelligence (AI) and machine learning

- Robotics and automation

- Voice-activated search

- Virtual and augmented reality

- 3D Printing

- Cyber security advances

- Software as a Service (SaaS) solutions

- The Work-from-Home Revolution

At the time of writing this revised edition of *ACCELERATE*, Openai.com (ChatGPT) is in its infancy, but make no mistake. It's disruptive. ChatGPT is a prototype artificial intelligence chatbot developed by OpenAI.com which specializes in dialogue type threaded search conversations. I brought my creative team into my conference room and said, "Mark my words, you've heard it here first, this is scary close to a sentient being, and I predict it's going to disrupt workforces, kill and create entire industries."

Huge Opportunities on the Horizon

I don't want you to focus on the challenges or get distracted. I just want you to know that I empathize with the challenges of growing a successful business. There is no shortage of opportunities. The super good news (does anybody else use that expression?) is that when you improve your marketing efforts and reduce the cost to acquire new customers, your profits increase. Remember, if money can fix it, it's a solvable problem.

Gain Total Clarity

Step back from working in your business and get the 30,000-foot view: On a scale of 1 to 10, with ten being a huge impact, what are your top three most significant challenges? If you're the owner reading this, ask your managers. Next, ask those closest to you, like your significant other, mastermind partners, and colleagues, for their ratings too.

The purpose is to get clarity on the area of focus that will benefit most from you using the highest and best use of your time. Stop stepping over dollars to pick up dimes. Procrastination and delusional thinking will steal your business success.

Jot down your Three Biggest Business Growth Challenges:

Chapter 3: The Hard Truth

Do you want the good news or the bad news?

Let's start with the bad news. The challenges you defined in Chapter 2 may not be your biggest problems. Sure, all of those I listed are at play in today's economy, but if your business isn't where you want it to be, it's not just because of buyer behaviors, competition, generational differences, or anything else you may feel is the cause.

Maybe I should've said the good news, bad news, and worse news.

The worse news is that if your business isn't where you want it to be, it's up to you and your team to make a difference.

Buying into these "challenges" can show up in a few different ways:

- Playing the victim

- Blaming

- Complaining

- Making excuses

- Procrastination

What's the one thing they all have in common? Deferring accountability. It's not your fault that business isn't going well. Sales are down because of COVID, the political climate, who's in the White House, too many competitors… insert your favorite scapegoat.

Are you still there, or did you throw the book across the room while cursing my name?

But there's good news! (And we'll get to it in a minute.)

As a franchisee, you may feel that the franchisor (corporate brand) should be doing more to drive brand awareness and traffic to your business. If you're part of a retail location business model, you want more walk-in traffic and new and repeat sales.

If you're a services business brand, you want more leads and new and repeat sales. Like many franchise opportunities, a percentage of every sale you make may go into a national co-op advertising fund or help support national advertising campaigns, so why is it that your phone isn't ringing off the hook and there isn't a line of customers pounding down your doors?

Let's look at this from the franchisor's point of view.

The founders created the business model and then turned it into their franchise brand opportunity. You purchased that branded system and became a franchisee.

While I'm not speaking on behalf of any specific franchise brand directly, I can say with little doubt that they feel if you're not as successful as you want to be with your business, it's because you're not fully utilizing their resources, following their marketing plans, working with preferred vendors, and taking enough of the right actions on a consistent basis.

Again, my words not theirs. So, if you got this book as a gift after my keynote presentation or book signing, please don't blame them. These are my observations and opinions after decades of working in the franchise industry.

Franchise Relations.

As a franchisee, it's important to recognize the value of a strong franchise relationship with your franchisor. This partnership plays a big role in your success.

I'm not trying to kick a hornet's nest because I've been around the block enough years in franchising to know the horror stories from both the franchisor and franchisee's perspective.

The point is that effective communication is crucial in maintaining a healthy franchisor/franchisee relationship. Whoever's reading this book, please be open to changes, and be proactive towards resolving any issues.

I mention the topic of "franchise relations" because too often, local franchisees get distracted from putting their efforts into what they can control, which is their local marketing and sales efforts, versus what's out of their control.

As I'll be reminding you, the reader, throughout this book, just in case you skipped ahead, it's **important to adhere to the terms of the franchise agreement and represent the brand consistently**.

By following the guidelines set forth by your franchisor and working together, you can build a successful business and achieve your entrepreneurial goals. Remember, a strong franchise relationship is key to your success as a franchisee.

Honesty time. The power is in our own hands.

You've undoubtedly heard the saying, "You can lead a horse to water, but you can't make them drink." Well, an essential part of franchise success is taking 100% responsibility for your actions and inactions, your performance, and your results.

Don't reinvent the wheel.

Review your brand's essential business systems, processes, and procedures. Building on the theme of the previous chapter, please take a hard look at your business operations and what you and your team do every day.

Think about how you'd answer these questions:

1. Am I taking full responsibility and accountability for my success?

2. Am I consistently making the most of the instructional training tools and portal access provided to me during the onboarding phase of my franchise purchase?

3. Are we actively and consistently following my brand's systems?

4. Am I proactive with our local area marketing and sales efforts?

5. Do I attend and take advantage of my brand's annual convention, regional conferences, and training webinars?

Block out time on your calendar to review and prioritize the training modules provided by your franchise brand and identify who else on your team needs to go through or review them.

Reading is great… Acting is better. Please download your *ACCELERATE* Companion Study Guide at

www.FranchiseTrainingSolutions.com/accelerate-tool-kit.

Chapter 4: Positivity Mindset: Because Negativity is So Last Year

Let's get back to you now. How many times have you uttered the following words, "I'm not a salesperson" or "I'm not a marketer" or "I don't have time to market"?

It turns out that the biggest predictor of whether or not you're a success in business… is whether or not you believe you'll be a success in business.

There's a good chance that you went into your business because you're passionate about your products or services, wanted to be an entrepreneur, and take control of your destiny. What you may not have been ready for was marketing, selling, leading staff, and operational responsibilities that you need to do, manage, or delegate as a franchise business owner.

I get it.

As I mentioned before, there are three strength skill set categories in running a successful business.

Three Skill Set Areas of Successful Franchisees:

Marketing and Selling — You know how to promote and sell.

Operations — You are skilled at delivering a product or service offering, including providing exceptional customer experiences while leading and managing everything on the customer journey.

Financial Management — You are skilled at managing bookkeeping (looking backwards using accounting best practices) and financial planning (looking forward, making strategic data-driven decisions).

Here's another hard truth:

Which skill set category areas are you strongest? While ideally, you'd be strong in all of them, the truth is you're only truly strong in one or two areas. Focus on leveraging your strengths and hire out your weaknesses.

Go ahead, hire the right help, but it's essential for you to understand and communicate what success looks like and set clear outcomes, expectations, and goals. Then ensure that you have processes in place to measure performance and improve accountability.

Local marketing is a critical link in the chain of growing your franchise business. Your product or service is important but not nearly as important as your ability to spread the word through targeted local marketing efforts. We'll get to the specific tactics soon. I promise.

Consider this: how many terrible restaurants have waiting lists around dinner time? That's not a good product, that's good marketing. How many great restaurants have gone out of business?

Those business owners probably blamed everything from the franchisor to the economy to the price of salmon on a Sunday morning. But the actual fault belongs to the marketing (or lack thereof).

Telling yourself that you aren't a marketer or aren't a salesperson, that's just creating a belief for yourself — a false and harmful belief. What if I had told myself that I wasn't a painter? What if I believed that I wasn't an entrepreneur? Even worse, what if I was convinced that I *was* worthless?

Replace Negative Beliefs with Empowering Beliefs

As franchisees, we understand firsthand how hard it can be to stay motivated when faced with unexpected challenges along our business journey — but what if there was a way to frame those struggles as opportunities instead?

Throughout this book, we'll discuss actionable steps that you can take to cultivate your own positive mindset and help reach your goals. So read on to uncover the secrets of finding fulfillment through facing adversity head on!

Accelerated Growth System™

I'd like to introduce you to Peter. He had always been a successful entrepreneur. He prided himself on his ability to run an efficient franchise location, and he was confident that his success would only continue to grow.

For a while, he had more business demand than he could serve. But when the market began to shift, Peter found himself struggling for the first time ever in his business career. He started cutting back on marketing expenses, stopped going to networking events, and was experiencing high staff turnover. His attitude was changing for the worse, and he found himself frustrated and short-tempered way too much.

He felt like he tried all of the traditional methods of growing his business, but nothing seemed to be working. After doing some research, he discovered my *Accelerated Growth System™ (AGS)*.

It's the foundational program designed specifically for franchise owner-operators, like Peter, who needed help reigniting their passion and understanding of local area marketing and sales processes while still staying true to their brand's standards.

It's also the basis and byproduct of the concepts and tactics revealed in the book you're reading right now.

At first, Peter wasn't sure if it could really work, but as he started implementing what he learned about the power of a positive mindset from the AGS into his daily routines, this helped him reboot, recharge, and refocus his efforts in more empowering ways.

Things started turning around, and he was reenergized with a renewed passion for his franchise business. As it turned out, developing a positive mindset was essential for Peter's business growth! With its help, he finally felt back in control and ready to take on whatever challenges came next with confidence.

Having a positive mindset is key for achieving success in business and life, yet the constant obstacles of every day can weigh down even the most determined among us. But with focus, determination, and a well-crafted plan, it's possible to establish positive habits that promote an outlook full of optimism and possibilities.

Obstacles and difficult circumstances are a part of our lives.

A dozen tips we can use to develop a positive mindset and successful mental attitude.

1. Start by being open-minded and willing to be honest with yourself.

2. Exercise thankfulness and gratitude with your staff and customers. Send 5 thank-you or appreciation emails right now.

3. Create a Dream Board, aka Vision Board, and fill it with pictures that represent who you want to become, images that represent your dreams, and images that reflect your dream lifestyle. This isn't just about luxury items, it's about what we want to be, have, and do too.

4. Keep an appreciation diary.

5. Practice mindfulness by being present in the moment and letting go of negative thoughts.

6. Stay active and exercise regularly, as physical activity has a positive impact on mental health.

7. Spend time with people who are upbeat. Be proactive in building friendships and relationships. Work on getting the toxic and negative people out of your life.

8. Practice using constructive self-talk. We've discussed this in previous chapters. It's so important, it's worth repeating.

9. Determine the areas or beliefs where you experience negative patterns. Ask yourself better, more empowering questions, and you'll get more empowering results.

10. Every day, strive to smile more and make good impressions.

11. Join a mastermind group of success minded individuals that will call you out on your crap.

12. Establish your Success Library. More about that in a future chapter.

Chapter 5: Two Schools of Thought

After decades of entrepreneurial experience, I've discovered that there are two philosophies regarding marketing. You either belong to the first camp or the second.

1. Marketing is a necessary evil.

2. Marketing is a strategic weapon used to grow your business.

Would you like to take a quick guess as to which camp fares better in the business world?

If you guessed #2, you are correct. When you look at marketing as a necessary evil, you understand that it's something you have to or are supposed to do. You see it as someone else's responsibility.

Maybe you're the type that thinks you're delegating tasks to someone on your team, but what you may be doing is hiding your head in the sand and hoping someone else fixes your marketing challenges for you. That's not exactly empowering.

On the other hand, if you believe that marketing is a strategic weapon you can use to grow your business, you understand that marketing helps people. You know that you have the solution to your customer's problems, but to help them, you must let them know you exist.

All marketing is just communication. Selling is just communication. When you focus on understanding your customer's needs, and communicating your unique value, lead conversion increases and revenue increases.

While your product may not be curing diseases, let's put this in life-or-death terms to really drive this point home. If you have the antidote to a poison that would bring someone back from the brink of death... but no one knows that your company exists or that you have a product that can save lives... does it really matter that you exist at all?

Let me answer that for you. It doesn't. A few years ago, I lost my son, Logan, age 27, to cancer. If someone out there had been able to save him, I would've wanted to know about them.

One of my all-time favorite quotes is from P.T. Barnum, "Without marketing, a terrible thing happens... nothing."

Let's take a look at some other beliefs you have that may not be serving your business.

"Everyone is online these days. Traditional marketing doesn't work anymore."

Well, what if I told you that it's *because* everyone is online *that* traditional marketing works now even better. In fact, because the social media landscape is so saturated, tactics like direct mail, local canvasing, and networking are incredibly powerful tactics for local businesses.

We'll dig deeper on how to leverage those and more in future chapters. For now, I just want you to realize that false beliefs due to negative past programming may be standing in the way of your success.

"Social Media is saturated, and I don't need to be on platforms like Facebook, YouTube, Instagram, Twitter, etc."

Do you know why they are saturated? Because that's where people (i.e., prospects and customers) spend time. And when looking for solutions, they're going to search online. That's why having a strong local online presence, aka digital footprint, is so important.

Online is one of the first places they'll look for information about your business, and if you aren't visible or findable on these platforms and in search engines, they'll stop looking.

"I've built my business on referrals. I don't need to do any other marketing."

Congratulations. Building your business on referrals is cost effective, shortens the sales cycle, and helps increase sales. However, if you're solely relying on referrals, it's most likely because you're not effectively executing local marketing campaigns and new customers aren't calling or walking through your door from any other source.

Would it be terrible if a customer found you another way? Would you turn them away? Of course not. Do you know your cost to acquire a new customer? In a previous chapter we discussed how local marketing is an investment, and not an expense. As my friend, Harvey Mackay, says, "Dig your well before you're thirsty." Supplementing your referral efforts with ongoing local marketing is a formula for success.

"I don't need to speak to my customers when I'm making decisions about my business. That's what my team is for."

Ummm. Is your team your ideal customer (which we'll discuss in a later chapter)? If your team wouldn't actually buy your product, they probably don't have the most useful opinions. Not to mention that depending on your relationship with them, they may agree with anything you say.

Don't create in a vacuum, stay in tune, ask your customers how else you can serve them, and align your local marketing messages and strategies accordingly.

"I prefer not to spend time focused on KPIs or analytics."

When I hear people say this, it's usually code for, "I'm too scared to look at my performance and financial numbers, and I know they aren't good, so I'll just hide my head in the sand and ignore them." This. Won't. Help.

There's one more concept we have to tackle before we move away from the mindset chapter. Now, I'm actually going to give you the benefit of the doubt here. I think that the mere fact that you picked up this book and are reading it, means that you don't suffer from this mindset challenge. But bear with me anyway as I think it may help you help your team.

No matter what audience I speak to, there's always at least one person leaning back in their seat, arms folded across their chest, face frozen in an irritated grimace. Their body language (and the dirty looks they're shooting me) communicate one thing very clearly…

"I've heard this or these concepts all before."

My first thought is, "Sure maybe you've heard it before, but have you formed your judgments through real experience or just speculation?" In fact, I've had clients sitting in my office at Prime Concepts, a Full-Service Creative Marketing Agency, verbalizing it.

Then they add something to the effect of "I've tried it before, and it didn't work" or "That will never work for me or my business because…" Then they argue with me about their limitations.

I want to be totally transparent with you. I can't help people who are close-minded, negative, or seriously infected with victimhood mentality. Maybe they weren't always living in fear or full of negative conditioning or fixated in the old way of doing things that has been ingrained in their psyche.

If they're not open-minded, coachable, or haven't experienced enough pain yet, they won't be open to change and adapt new ideas, strategies, and tactics.

In a previous chapter, I mentioned that I'll be sharing some wisdom with you that you may have already heard. I also stated (quite a few times and I'm just getting started) that *it's not what you know, it's how well you execute*.

If you've tried any of these techniques discussed in this book before and they haven't worked, I'm willing to bet that it's because:

    a.   Fears, negativity, or delusional thinking prevented you from taking action or

    b.   You didn't execute them properly and make the necessary adjustments or

    c.   You stopped too soon. You didn't execute long enough to get any traction.

As we wrap up this chapter, I want to congratulate you again on your commit to learn, adapt, and grow!

Whenever I conduct my business growth summit events, that are multi-day events with tickets starting at $5,000 or more to attend, I ask them to create (and agree to) a PERSONAL COMMITMENT STATEMENT.

A **personal commitment statement** is a statement that outlines a specific goal and the steps that an individual (that would be you) are willing to take in order to achieve that goal. It is a way to commit to our goals and to set us up for success.

A personal commitment statement for goal setting might look something like this:

"I am committed to achieving my goal of (insert specific goal here). I am willing to take the following steps to achieve this goal: (list specific steps here). I understand that achieving this goal will take time and effort, but I am dedicated to putting in the work to make it happen. I am confident in my ability to succeed, and I am determined to do whatever it takes to reach my goal." _____

Before we go any further, I'm asking you to do the same below or in your *ACCELERATE* Companion Guide. Thanks!

"I _____ am committed to achieving my goal(s) of *(insert specific goal(s) here)*.

I am willing to take the following steps to achieve this goal(s)::

I understand that achieving this goal will take time and effort, but I am dedicated to putting in the work to make it happen. I am confident in my ability to succeed, and I am determined to do whatever it takes to reach my goal."

Signed _____   Date _____

ACCELERATE

Chapter 6: Time? What's that? I'm Too Busy Not Having It!

I don't have time for one more thing in my business or life!

"Ford, you don't understand. I'm so busy working in my business, I don't have time to work on my business."

Sound familiar? Michael Gerber made a similar statement famous in his book titled *The E-Myth*, and it's been echoed by entrepreneurs and business owners for decades.

It may seem like hard work, dedication, and long hours are the only ingredients for success, but sometimes even the strongest of us get caught up in merely tending to day-to-day operations with limited time or resources to plan strategically and work on local marketing.

For all you franchisees out there who feel like you're constantly working in your businesses not on them — this book is for you! We'll be discussing best practices and practical strategies that will help make your life easier and maximize efficiency.

This will allow you to have more headspace to focus on executing big-picture strategies, following your systems, and developing your local marketing and sales playbook so you can win big!

But first, let's address the elephant in the room. If you reclaimed the time you spend on lower priority activities, poor habits, or distractions, you'd have more time to focus on your local marketing and selling efforts.

Mindset. Is your self-talk and first response when you think about local area marketing, prospecting, or selling, "I don't have time?" If so, my advice to you is to consider saying, "It's not a priority" instead and see how that feels.

I was honored to present at Orangetheory Fitness® franchises annual conference on accelerating sales performance. During the interaction portion of my keynote, a franchise owner raised his hand, and said, "These are wonderful concepts, but we don't have time to spend on them with all of our other responsibilities." I asked them, "When your studio customers cancel their memberships, is it because you have an inferior service or that the customer doesn't have time to attend your fitness classes?" "No, they have the time, it's just not a priority."

I know, because I'm an OTF member and have fallen victim to the "I don't have time to work out" myth too at times. Orangetheory® offers early morning classes I can make if I don't stay up too late at night doing research, writing books, watching TV, or yes, at times, scrolling through social media.

I get it. As I mentioned, I've been an entrepreneur for over 40 years, with over 10 of my own companies, having hired hundreds of employees. I sit on several advisory boards of associations and corporations made up of entrepreneurs, executives, and owners.

Having worked with literally thousands of business owners and top brands in franchising and small and medium sized businesses, it's common to fall into the trap of feeling like you're being pulled in multiple directions all at the same time.

We all make time for what's important in our lives. Being busy is an epidemic these days.

Ask Yourself:

- Are busy being effective or efficient?

- Are you constantly distracted with interruptions, from your staff, customers, mobile phone notices, and desktop alerts?

- Are you stressed trying to put out fires and feeling overwhelmed?

- Are you focused on the highest priorities and best use of your time?

Chapter 7: Becoming a Time Bandit

Steal Back Minutes and Hours from Your Busy Day

Do you want to be better at managing your time and becoming more productive?

Silly question, of course you do. Let's make room in your busy life so you can invest your time on local area marketing, creating amazing customer experiences, and accelerate your business growth!

Here are a dozen ways to reclaim your time.

1. Follow your brand's systems.

A huge part of being a successful franchisee is understanding how important it is to stick to proven systems and procedures set forth by your brand's parent company. Following tried-and-tested methods ensures reliability, efficiency, and consistency across all locations — thus driving success for both the franchisor and franchisees alike.

Don't waste time reinventing the wheel. Stay current on your brand's training systems, online courses, newsletters, and virtual meetings. Attend your regional and national conventions and go with the purpose of building relationships with other owners so you can share best practices and stay current on trends in your industry.

2. Be mindful of your self-talk.

Many people find it hard to stay on top of their tasks, often blaming outside circumstances or their own lack of discipline. However, a powerful yet overlooked factor that affects time management is positive self-talk. It can significantly influence your attitude and productivity levels so it's important to be mindful of what thoughts you cultivate to ensure they are working in your favor.

Your self-talk affects your relationship with time and can create patterns you find yourself repeating, both negative and positive... it's your choice.

Here are a couple simple tricks that you can use immediately. Say "get to" instead of "have to." Creating positive affirmations like "you've got this," "you can do it," or "keep going" can boost your confidence.

Break the pattern of asking negative questions or inner dialogue. Avoid mentally asking, "Why does this happen to me?" and replace it with a more empowering question like, "How can I make this better?" Focus on what you can control, which is your attitude and your actions.

3. Blocked time slots on your calendar.

Blocking time slots for each of your high-priority activities will provide structure and clarity so you can get done what needs to be done in a timely manner. Determine your high-priority activities and evaluate how much time you estimate is needed to complete them.

Block out time slots (blocks) on your calendar for each activity, along with time limits for how long you will work on a task before taking a break. I use my Zoho CRM and Outlook calendars with color coding and set timers using Alexa. Another favorite is Acuity Online Scheduler. I use it to share links with direct access to my calendar to help set up meetings and avoid email and phone tag craziness.

There are numerous apps and websites designed to help you improve your focus, organization, and time management skills, but don't get seduced by technology. Find what works for you. Stick to the schedule as best you can. Review your progress periodically and make necessary adjustments. Celebrate your successes!

4. Reduce and remove distractions.

Identify the distractions that rob your time and prevent you from being more productive. Turn off the news. Limit your TV time. Clean up your desk and working environment. Create a plan to deal with potential distractions when they inevitably come up.

Stick to your plan and be consistent in your efforts to stay focused. Replace your distractions with higher-productive use of your time. It takes practice. Aim for improvement, not perfection.

5. Silence alerts.

Being a successful franchise owner requires plenty of focus, but it can be incredibly challenging to stay focused and productive when you're constantly interrupted by phone and desktop alerts. Whether they're coming from social media updates, emails, your smartphone, your web browser, or other notifications, those unwanted distractions can quickly pull you away from the task at hand.

Research shows that those little alert interruptions cause you to lose your train of thought, reduce comprehension, and it can take 5 to 8 minutes for your brain to refocus on what you were doing before the alert.

Do the math on that one, and you'll quickly see why you may feel like you don't have time. Fortunately, silencing all of these distracting alerts is easy. Go to your device settings or the specific application and turn them off. You'll easily find videos on YouTube on how to silence any unwanted alert or notification.

Exception: If you're the one who answers the phone or responds to website inquiries, then leave those alerts ON. It's essential that you respond quickly to leads because your prospects are most likely sitting in front of their phone or computer searching for solutions, and the faster you respond, the more likely you'll get the sale.

6. Control interruptions.

Do you ever feel like the day is slipping away and you can't stay focused or on-task? It can be difficult to remain productive when unexpected interruptions continually pull us away from our important activities.

As a franchisee, it can be even more challenging maintaining productivity with inconsistent customer demands and business operations that require your full attention. It's challenging, but not impossible, to avoid interruptions. Legitimate interruptions are unavoidable. You must take care of them right now; you have no other option. Making the distinction between legitimate and invalid interruptions is a simple method to increase your productivity and well-being.

Another great way to help reduce interruptions is to identify repeatable interruptions, and then create short videos to answer common questions. Then post the videos on YouTube or Vimeo and mark them unlisted or private.

Then create a templated email or landing page with the titles of the topic and links to the videos, or embed them, that you can use to help answer requests instead of getting interrupted or use the videos to help reduce the time it takes to address the interruption. Yes, you still have to make time to record and publish the videos, but the short-term effort provides you with long-term repeatable benefits.

7. Leverage the 80/20 rule — the Pareto Principle.

Vilfredo Pareto, an Italian economist, "discovered" this principle in 1897, and it's as applicable today as it was then. The rule can be applied to our own productivity in that 80% of our outcomes come from 20% of our efforts.

Test this. I bet that 20% of your marketing produces 80% of your leads. 20% of your product or service offerings produce 80% of your sales. And that 20% of your staff or customers cause 80% of your headaches. You get the point.

The challenge is to identify that 20% that produces positive results so that we can concentrate the majority of our efforts there and reduce efforts on the remaining 80% that does not deliver the desired results.

8. Be specific and set clear outcomes.

Knowing how to set effective goals is critical to achieving successful outcomes. With clearly defined objectives, you can develop a team that is organized and focused on delivering the desired targets. But when it comes down to performance management, many of us forget one of the most important elements: specificity.

As an entrepreneur, I'm a problem solver and critical thinker. I've been a business consultant for decades trained to identify problems, find solutions, and transform results.

For years, I found myself struggling with getting my staff to improve productivity and accountability. Why are they wasting so much time? Why are they doing it wrong? Why is it so difficult to find good leaders and team members? (Before you blast me on how that may be negative self-talk... stay with me.)

The issues to improve performance includes two main intertwined components. First, we needed to hire right, train to standard, and put systems in place for procedures and accountability. Secondly, we needed to ensure that we were specific in our communication, set clear outcomes, and implemented processes to drive accountability.

My challenge was that I thought everyone had common sense and could solve problems like I do, but sadly, that's delusional thinking. I was also delusional in thinking that I was communicating clearly. I still struggle with **"delegating without details only ends with disasters."** There's a tweet for you, just attribute it to me. Thanks.

Moving on. I take 100% responsibility for everything in my business and had to discover many lessons the hard way. The concept of styles was crystalized when I read Gino Wickman's book, *Traction: Get a Grip on Your Business*. Visionaries tend to operate more on emotion than on logic and strongly value the company culture. Visionaries offer integrators a creative insight to the business, while integrators provide the logical and structured approach that is also needed.

I'm absolutely a visionary, and I've trained my staff to ensure they get the details they need to effectively perform their responsibilities. We have our WORKING STANDARDS for Prime Concept Group, our creative marketing agency guidelines printed on posters in our offices, and each workstation has a mouse pad with the primary questions they need to ask BEFORE starting a project.

Those questions help ensure they get the specific outcomes on what does success look like?

Have we solved this problem before?

Do we have an SOP?

What resources can we reference?

Do we need Ford's strategic brain for clarification?

Then they are encouraged to create standard operating procedures (SOPs) for repeatable tasks. We create our SOPs in word documents and create short training/SOP videos using Loom.com and have them indexed and accessible to our entire team. This also helps with the onboarding and training of new staff members too.

By taking the time to get specific with expectations and setting clear goals, we can ensure that everyone understands what needs to be accomplished — resulting in improved productivity and performance across all areas of business operations. As a franchisee, you have access to a variety of SOPs. Now's a great time to revisit what's available to you through your head office.

9. Focus on high-value priorities — big rocks.

As a franchisee, staying focused on the big rocks — or most important tasks — of your work can help keep things flowing smoothly.

The big rocks concept of "If the big rocks don't go in first, they aren't going to fit in later" was popularized in Steven Covey's book, *The 7 Habits of Highly Effective People.* Big rocks refer to making time for your high-value priorities and initiatives.

As a franchisee, I know you wear many hats and have plenty of demands on your time. It's easy to get overwhelmed when faced with such a wide range of tasks, but setting priorities is the key to success. Knowing which issues demand your attention now and which ones can wait until later allows you to make the most efficient use of your energy and resources.

Here's a reminder of the four levels of tasks — the Eisenhower Matrix.

- Urgent and important. Tasks that require immediate attention. Do these FIRST.

- Important, but not urgent. Tasks that can be SCHEDULED.

- Urgent, but not important. DELEGATE these tasks to others.

- Neither urgent nor important. Distraction tasks. DELETE or reduce these activities.

It's critical that you start with your goals, vision, and mission to ensure that your priorities have a purpose. Start the prioritizing process by doing a brain dump of all your tasks.

Then sort and categorize them into buckets, like marketing and sales, operations, production, accounting, HR, etc. Next, estimate and allocate time requirements for each task.

Then look at the list and ask yourself which of these items will produce the highest results and order them accordingly. Plan for the unexpected.

Then execute, track your performance, make the necessary course corrections, and then repeat what works. Once you have the formula, document it by turning it into an SOP.

10. Leverage technology solutions.

Embracing the right technology not only streamlines daily processes but also strengthens customer relationships and drives business success. Technology can be a double-edged sword. It's essential for keeping your business competitive in today's digital age.

But as useful as technology may be, it also presents unique challenges which could stand in the way of continued success if not addressed appropriately. This topic may seem a bit counter intuitive since I told you to silence alerts and control interruptions, but this time saver refers to using the right and approved technology in the form of smartphone apps and online software solutions.

What systems and technology has your franchise brand made available to you? On a scale of 1 to 10, with 10 being best, how effective are you and your team in leveraging that technology?

This includes your accounting system, CRM, point-of-sale, website portal, web app, and your other branded proprietary systems.

Remember, I'm not setting policy or suggesting you go rogue and add in new technology, so please check with corporate before you implement any new technology and stay within your compliance guidelines.

This topic goes deeper into chatbots, marketing automation, self-driving cars, voice search and automation, Artificial Intelligence (AI) devices like Alexa and Siri, AI driven web applications, SaaS systems like Google Suite and Microsoft Office, and more just to name a few.

Here's a few of my favorite productivity technology solutions:

- Microsoft 365® Suite — Office.com. We utilize the entire suite, including Outlook, Word, Excel, PowerPoint, Access, and OneNote.

- Accuity Appointment Scheduling — acuityscheduling.com. This is my online calendar for prospects and clients. Grab a meeting with me using www.15withford.com. I'd love to meet with you 1-on-1 to help you address your top challenges. I share that link on podcasts to make it easy to connect with potential customers.

- Slack.com — a messaging app for teams and groups. We use it for our agency, and also for my other mastermind groups.

- Zoho.com — our CRM system for managing marketing automation and sales activities.

- Zoom Meetings and Webinars — hardly needs explaining after the pandemic. We love face-to-face meetings and having the ability to record and review the video and transcripts definitely has improved productivity.

- Canva.com — quick graphic design tool. Especially useful when my graphic designer is busy.

- LastPass.com — Secure every one of your passwords and store them across all of your devices. Protect every access point while seamlessly connecting employees to their work.

- Teamwork.com — our online project management system our creative agency uses to manage and centralize communication, organize tasks, and track performance.

Again, don't get seduced by shiny object syndrome. Use critical thinking. Test and track the performance of your technology and measure those results to help identify and deploy technology solutions.

11. Expand personal development.

Seems almost silly to mention this tip because you wouldn't be reading this book or going through the exercises if you weren't interested in improving your performance and results.

A Success Library is comprised of resources in print, digital, video, and audio formats with topics that are most required for the success of your business and used to improve your quality of life.

I'm honored and want to thank you again for including the *ACCELERATE* book and the online companion resources into your Success Library. What other resources do you have to help you and your team improve their skill sets, productivity, and performance?

Start by identifying the skill sets necessary for the different roles and areas of your business. Once you have the list, the next step is to add resources to your Success Library and your brain. Think about what courses, consultants, or how-to training resources will best help you bridge your value gap. You're building more than a bookshelf.

Your Success Library is any and all of the resources you need, in whatever medium (mentors, consultants, audiobooks, podcasts, videos, online courses) you can find to support your business growth and personal success journey. Success leaves clues. You can either learn from your own experience or from other people's experiences. Why reinvent the wheel when you can shorten your learning curve through the guidance of successful people?

As a business, you'll improve engagement and retention when you give your staff opportunities for knowledge and skills growth by providing Success Library resources. It could be onboarding videos about your company's culture, standard operating procedures, or the customer experience you cultivate. Or it could be about the mentors you tap or the experts you bring to your business for skills training.

For example, when I speak at a franchise conference or training event, I become a part of its Success Library. I've added value, given them tools, techniques, templates, guidelines, formulas, and stories they can relate to with actionable takeaways.

Everyone can benefit from a Success Library. There is no end of information out there to tap into to gain insights and glean value. There are no excuses.

12. Celebrate success.

Madison was an ambitious franchise owner with a dream to become a multi-unit owner having at least 5 locations in the next 3 years. She opened her first location, had the right team, and plenty of determination but still found it difficult to stay motivated. Each time she encountered an obstacle in her journey, Madison felt like giving up and letting the dream slip away.

One day while attending my business growth presentation, Madison was reminded of the advice on celebrating successes no matter how small they may be. I had emphasized that acknowledging each win along the way will help keep your motivation levels high, even when faced with challenges or obstacles that can seem insurmountable at times.

This message resonated deeply with Madison, and she decided to start implementing it right away. As soon as she achieved something new (big or small), she took some time for herself to celebrate this milestone — whether that meant going out for dinner with friends, taking a weekend getaway or simply treating herself to something special!

By doing this regularly and allowing herself space in between wins to appreciate what she had accomplished so far, Madison began noticing huge differences in her attitude toward her franchise business as well as increased productivity levels overall!

It seemed like every success story was paving the way for another one and before long, her hard work paid off: In less than two years from launching her first location, Madison's dream of being a profitable multi-unit franchisee came true!

Madison now knows firsthand why it is important to take regular breaks from working hard and recognize your successes along the way — not only does celebrating give you much-needed rewards but also provides you with renewed energy so that you are ready to tackle whatever lies ahead of you on your entrepreneurial path!

Every small step along your journey that is moving you toward your ultimate goal is a reason to celebrate.

Here are a few great ways to celebrate your success: *(Excerpted from my SUPERPOWER book.)*

- Go to a day spa.
- Take a vacation.
- Go shopping.
- Play a musical instrument.

- Take a walk in the park.
- Read a fiction book.
- Connect with your friends.
- Take dance lessons.
- Capture the moment with photos.
- Record and post a video to YouTube.
- Pay to get your house cleaned.
- Buy flowers.
- Go for a run.
- Go to the gym.
- Walk your dog.
- Send thank-you cards to everyone who supported you.
- Go out to a movie.
- Spend the day with your family.
- Go to a concert or play.
- Attend a sporting event.
- Tweet your accomplishment.
- Listen to the radio.
- Take a nap.
- Go out dancing.
- Have a party.
- Spend a day in total silence.

Celebrating your success is much more than just telling other people about it. It's recognizing any progress on your journey toward your goals.

If all you ever do is focus on the negative or the problems in your life and ignore the positive, this will undoubtedly derail your dreams and motivation to succeed.

Focusing only on the negative and not rewarding yourself for the positive will chip away at your self-confidence. Stop and ask yourself, "What are three things I did right today?"

In summary:

1. Please follow your systems and brand guidelines.

2. Be mindful of your self-talk.

3. Block time on your calendar.

4. Remove distractions.

5. Silence your unnecessary alerts.

6. Control interruptions.

7. Leverage the 80/20 rule.

8. Set and communicate clear outcomes.

9. Focus on your "big rock" priorities.

10. Leverage technology solutions.

11. Expand personal development.

12. Celebrate success.

PART II — EFFECTIVE MARKETING MANAGEMENT

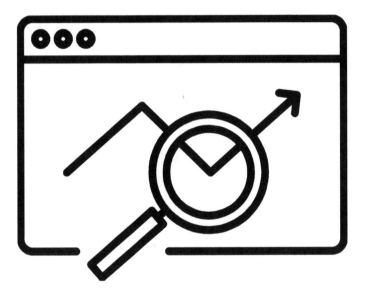

Chapter 8: Goal Digging

How to Set Your Sights on Success and Unearth Profits in Your Business

Where Are You Now and Where Would You Like to Go? (Setting Goals and KPIs.)

It was my third year of my sporting goods manufacturing business. I was only 23 years old. I had invented and patented bicycle storage solutions, oak and aluminum pole systems that allowed people to store multiple bikes in limited spaces, without drilling holes into the walls or ceilings.

Frankly, I thought I was crushing it. I got serious, throwing on my proverbial horse blinders and focused on generating revenue through multiple channels of distribution. Retail direct, mass merchants, wholesale, distributers, chain stores, and more.

It worked. I generated over 1 million dollars in sales that year. (Cue the cheering!)

When I walked into my accountant's office, I was on top of the world. I was prepared to receive his highest praise, ready to bow after a job well done, and all set to celebrate with a nice dinner that night with my wife.

"Hold on there, skippy," said my accountant after I began the conversation by congratulating myself. "You may have generated 1 million dollars in sales, but you're $150k in debt, and you took a salary of $16,000. That's less than minimum wage."

It looked like my wife and I would be celebrating with cheap TV dinners.

My accountant continued, "It's not about what you earn, Ford. It's about what you keep."

Right about now, you might be wondering what happened. How did I create such an epic failure while thinking I was succeeding?

I set my sights on the wrong goal.

My goal for my business was to create at least 1 million dollars in sales, but in the process, I didn't realize how poorly I was managing the other aspects of my business. When we set the wrong goals, or even worse, don't set any goals at all, we end up focused on the wrong things, wasting money, and executing poorly.

Proper, well-structured goals serve as a guiding star for our business. Only once we've determined where we're going can we plan our strategy to get there.

Setting SMART Goals is a widely used framework for setting goals that are clear, actionable, and achievable.

Most likely you've encountered this goal setting strategy. In case it's been a while, let's do a quick recap of the acronym SMART.

1. Specific - be very clear on what it is you want to achieve and why.

2. Measurable - quantifiable goals allow you to track your progress and stay motivated.

3. Actionable - are the necessary steps within your control? You must be able to take specific actions to reach your goal.

4. Relevant - make sure that the goal actually matters. Does it align with your other goals? Is it important to you at this time?

5. Time Measured - when do you need to accomplish the goal by? Are there smaller, incremental steps that can be used as goals with the eventual desired outcome in sight?

You have to know where you are going if you have any hope of getting there. You want to be successful, of course. But what does success look like to you? It's not the same for everyone.

For some, success may be building a 7-billion-dollar company no matter the cost to their personal life. For others, success could look like a million-dollar business that affords the owner time to spend with his or her family and friends.

For another business owner, success may look like building a thriving company that treats its employees fairly, gives back to the community, and uses all "green" materials to manufacture their products.

My point is success is not a one-size-fits-all end game. In order to achieve it, you have to first figure out what you want and define it in writing. How will you know when you've reached this mythical state of "success"? And why do you want to reach this place?

Business is hard. It requires long hours, sacrifice, money, energy, blood, sweat, and tears. If you don't know why you're doing what you're doing, you won't have anything to focus on when the days are difficult. If your reasons for wanting the goal aren't big enough, your excuses will be.

When writing SMART Goals, use concise language but include relevant information. These are designed to help you succeed, so be positive when answering the questions.

Goals Feed and Fuel Motivation

I like to separate goals strategically into three different categories:

Big goals: What does your ultimate success look like, how will you measure it, why is it important to you, and what's your big picture vision and mission for clarity?

Long-term goals: These are targeted milestones 2 to 5 years into the future. Due to how fast economic, internal, and external forces are at play, reviewing your strategic plan and modifying your long-term goals accordingly, at least bi-annually, is a smart recommendation.

Short-term goals: What's your strategic and tactical plan, local area marketing calendar, and sales playbook items that you're going to execute monthly and for the next 24 months? As mentioned in a previous chapter, it's also important to celebrate the small wins as you strive for the big goals.

You need clear targets of where you want to go. Then you establish the milestones and reporting metrics, also known as Key Performance Metrics (KPIs) or Key Results (KRs), that you can use as guideposts to measure your progress. KPIs must be managed effectively if you want to develop and track the performance of your franchise business. To accomplish this in your franchise's decentralized environment, you must first consider which metrics you want to use to gauge the effectiveness of your location(s).

Financial Reporting and MTOs

Once your goals are clearly fleshed out, written down, and shared with your entire team, you'll have clarity of focus and targets to hit. I know this is a book about local marketing and selling, but you can't manage what you aren't measuring. I think that came from Peter Drucker, but the concept is true.

Goals are intertwined with knowing where you currently are and understanding the KPIs in your business. While most businesses have to create KPIs on their own, you are at an advantage. As a franchisee, your franchisor has already done the work for you. They have multiple stores selling the same thing and have put these standards and insights into a set of numbers for you to work with.

They can provide you with your MTO numbers: Minimal, Target, and Optimal, to benchmark your store(s) with the rest of the franchise.

If you own a QSR franchise, they'll tell you that the average store makes $1 million per year. Maybe your goal is to make $2 million per year. It may be doable, but it's good to know how other stores with similar market territories are doing.

Like any business, you'll need to keep accurate financial records as these will act as a report card for the success of your business. I won't go into bookkeeping here, but suffice to say, you'll be reviewing balance sheets and income statements throughout the benchmarking process and throughout the life of your business.

If you don't want to do this, make sure you have someone who is comfortable in this role (and trustworthy). And just because you don't want to handle it, doesn't mean you shouldn't still be aware of everything that's going on. This is the lifeblood of your business and shouldn't be left to chance.

*** *Download this from the Companion Tool Kit* ***

S.M.A.R.T GOALS WORKSHEET

S **SPECIFIC**	What do you want to accomplish? Who needs to be included? When do you want to do this? Why is this a goal?
M **MEASURABLE**	How can you measure progress and know if you've successfully met your goal?
A **ACHIEVABLE**	Do you have the skills required to achieve the goal? If not, can you obtain them? What is the motivation for this goal? Is the amount of effort required on par with what the goal will achieve?
R **RELEVANT**	Why am I setting this goal now? Is it aligned with overall objectives?
T **TIME-BOUND**	What's the deadline and is it realistic?
SMART GOAL →	Review what you have written, and craft a new goal statement based on what the answers to the questions above have revealed.

Chapter 9: Financial KPIs for a Healthy Franchise

Moving on. Most likely you have a branded portal or tracking system that helps you measure your KPIs, accounting, and marketing analytics.

In this chapter we'll explore a few of the more important KPIs used for financial management.

Remember, accounting tracks transactions and the report data from your balance sheet and Profit & Loss report is focused on what's happened in the past. It's like looking in the rearview mirror to see where you've been.

Financial and strategic planning considers what's happened and the results of the past, allowing you to evaluate and then make changes for the future.

Here's a quick refresher to help keep you focused and profitable.

Gross Sales

Summary of your sales receipts for a given period. Gross sales is a crucial indicator, especially for franchise businesses, as it captures the total sales generated by a location over time and is helpful in identifying purchasing patterns, buyer behaviors, and seasonal spikes.

Gross Profit %

Gross profit can be measured in dollars and percentages. Take your sales minus your expenses, then divide that number by your total sales.

For example, (Sales of $20,000 - $10,000 in expenses)/Sales = Gross profit % of 50% (.50).

Net Profit %

Again, net profit can be measured in dollars and percentages. Total revenue minus total expenses equals your net profit. Use your Profit & Loss Report (P&L).

I like to export the data from my KPIs into excel sheets and create graphs measuring the changes from month to month because I'm a visual learner. This helps me see trends and adjust my strategic plan and tactics.

Sales By Category or Department

Calculate this by selecting the key categories you'd like to measure and print reports from your sales or accounting system. Measuring sales by category helps you determine where to focus your local marketing and sales efforts. Considerations for your customer journey and value-ladder must also be taken into consideration.

For example, franchise brands hire me as a keynote speaker. Then the franchise brand hires me as a franchise consultant to improve franchise relations or improve the way they generate new leads for new franchise owners. The franchise industry is very competitive, and prospective owners have lots of choices.

And then depending on the guidelines of each franchise brand, other regional or multi-unit owners will hire me for customized training on a variety of business growth topics.

So, my value-ladder includes, my podcast, keynotes, breakouts, custom on-site training services, franchise relations and strategic planning, sales funnel development, and done-for-you creative agency services for innovative campaigns. I track those sales by category, and that helps me plan my marketing and sales efforts throughout the entire customer journey.

Revenue Per Square Foot

This KPI applies if you have retail locations. It is a meaningful statistic to use to evaluate a store's performance and gives you and your manager insight into the effectiveness of the space in the store.

A store's revenue per square foot can provide useful information for merchandising, layout, staffing, and many other store improvements. Again, follow your brand's standards and guidelines.

Growth Rate — Period Over Period, Monthly and Annually

The growth rate KPI measures the rate of change in a company's financial or operational performance over a period of time. It is calculated by comparing the current period's performance to a previous period's performance.

For example, if a company's sales increased by 10% from one year to the next, its growth rate would be 10%.

At this point, you may be sitting back with an eyebrow raised thinking, "Ford, I told you at the beginning. I'm busy. In fact, I barely have time to read this book. Now you expect me to start running all of these reports **before** I can start marketing?"

I know it may seem daunting. Unfortunately, one of the biggest obstacles in a franchise is that you don't have enough talented people working for you.

Turnover is frequently high, and you may feel like you're so busy working on the front line trying to keep the customers happy (because you're so understaffed), that you don't think you have time to do anything else.

The thing is, the more effective marketing you do, the more (and better) people you can hire. It's a frustrating chicken and the egg scenario, but one that many businesses face.

Tracking and evaluating your KPIs will help drive your business. Without them, your business will drive you.

Make a list of your top financial KPIs and gather the financial data for at least the last 12 months.

What evaluations can you derive from the trends?

Are you on track, off track, or exceeding your expectations?

Chapter 10: Marketing & Sales Performance KPIs

Measuring the Success of Your Local Marketing Efforts

Let's continue exploring Key Performance Indicators that relate more towards Marketing and Sales performance. Sure, I could have just added them to the last chapter, but these are more relevant in measuring your local area marketing and selling efforts. Consider the complexity of your management team and divide up the KPI tracking and reporting accordingly.

It's a good practice to have your staff sign non-disclosures and confidentiality agreements if they have access to financial reports, marketing lists, or marketing metrics.

Check with your brand's corporate office for policies. And as a disclaimer, *This book, and all of its related content, is for educational and informational purposes only. I'm not giving you legal advice.* Okay, enough with the legalese...

Here's the list of marketing KPIs for your success dashboard.

Cost Per Acquisition (CPA)

Do you know your cost to acquire a new customer? The formula is straight forward. You take the entire cost of marketing over a given period of time and divide it by the total number of new customers in that same time period.

This is an important number for local advertising because without this KPI, you can't set your advertising, especially pay-per-click budgets.

You don't go broke making a profit, and you can lose money selling under your costs and expect to make it on volume. That dog doesn't hunt. Now, you can have products/services that you provide as a loss-leader, if you've calculated your conversion rates, average ticket value, and long-term value.

For example, being fully transparent, some associations, including the International Franchise Association (IFA), offer me speaking opportunities for their conferences and virtual events at discounted rates.

It makes sense for me, even as a hall of fame keynote speaker, research-based thought leader to occasionally accept discounted speaking fees because I want to increase my visibility in front of my ideal clients, which are franchise brand executives, franchisees, and vendors that serve the franchise industry.

These aren't infomercials trying to sell anything. They are opportunities to add value, be of service, and are in alignment with my mission, vision, and core values. I know if I deliver the value from the stage, that leads will naturally and organically come into my business.

Conversion Rates

Tracking your conversion rates from suspect to prospect, prospect reach to qualified leads, leads to sales, calls to appointments, proposals to sales, and sales to repeat purchases, average number of referrals per customer or by product/service, and long-term value are essential components to success with all traditional and digital local marketing mediums.

Here's the formula: the number of conversions (say visitors that completed a lead form/total appointments set x 100).

For example: if you get 100 people to inquire about your products/services, and 20 set appointments, it would be (20 leads/100 inquiries) x 100 = .2 or 20% conversion rate.

Average Transaction Value

The average transaction value KPI gives you insights into the average amount of sales per customer or employee. This metric is determined by adding up all of the sales during a certain period of time and dividing it by the total number of customers.

Total Sales/# of customers = avg. transaction value. Example, $50,000 in sales in JAN/200 customers in JAN = avg. transaction value of $250.

Lifetime Value of a Customer (LTV)

LTV is formulated by both real numbers and a data-driven estimated guess. You can track sales numbers of the total sales by customer to help you identify your rock star customers but tracking referrals from your customer advocates is a bit trickier.

We track referrals in our CRM system and work hard to grow our referral network. With a focus on delivering high-quality customer-centric experiences, you'll produce repeat sales and higher average tickets and generate referrals.

Local Territory Reach

Reach is measured in subscribers, prospect and customer lists, social media viewers, listeners, followers, and readers. What's your total local community reach? How many people do you have on your prospect and customer direct mailing lists? Have you pulled your social media metrics and entered them into an excel sheet or dashboard?

We use SEMrush to help our agency clients measure their reach and digital marketing performance. Your franchise system may have preferred vendors, and if so, make sure you get and review your marketing KPIs, especially your reach, frequency of messaging, the mediums, and conversion rates.

Comparable Location KPIs

This data will come from your head office, area developer, or regional manager to help you compare how you measure up against other franchisees in your category and franchise system.

I've worked with several Quick Service Restaurants (QSRs), fast-casual, and full-service dining brands. They use this metric to compare location KPIs based on the size of the territory or metropolitan population within a 5-mile radius. This metric only works if the criteria measured from location to location has similar attributes, otherwise it's not a helpful metric.

Net Promoter Score (NPS) - An Essential Customer Experience (CX) Metric

I saved this one for last in this chapter so we can take a deeper dive. Maybe you're already familiar with NPS, a system created by Fred Reichheld back in 2003. Many franchise brands have implemented NPS into their systems, so check with corporate to see if you already have access to a NPS system or preferred NPS vendor.

Even if you aren't familiar with the title NPS, you've no doubt been exposed to it if you purchased anything online through a major retailer.

That's where you get an email or pop-up or notice on the purchase thank-you page, asking you the ultimate question.

"On a scale of 1 to 10, with 10 being best, how likely is it that you'd refer _____ (insert company name) to one of your friends or colleagues?"

It's one question, although some brands have expanded it to more than one question, by asking follow-up questions like "Share your experience to help make us better."

Rating Your NPS Responses:

1. **Responders** who give a score of 1-6 are called **Detractors**. They are actively engaged to prevent people from doing business with you. This includes talking to friends and family and potentially posting negative comments on social media and review sites.

2. A score of 7-8 means you've got a **Passive Promoter**. They may recommend you, but only if they are directly asked about you.

3. Customers that rate a 9-10 are considered **Advocates**. They are the people that will be singing the praises of your brand. They are worth their weight in gold and creating advocates should be one of your top local marketing goals.

A high NPS (8 to 10) indicates that our company has a large number of satisfied and loyal customers, which is generally good for our business.

This is because satisfied and loyal customers are more likely to continue doing business with us, and they are also more likely to tell their friends and family about us, which can help to generate new customers.

Additionally, satisfied and loyal customers are less likely to switch to a competitor, which can help to increase a company's market share.

What's your Net Promoter Score?

To execute a NPS survey, follow these steps:

1. **Determine the goal** of the survey and the target audience. For example, you might want to survey customers who have purchased a particular product or service, or you might want to survey all of your customers.

2. Choose a **survey platform** or tool. There are many options available, including online survey tools, email survey tools, and survey apps. ** Check with your brand's preferred vendors. **

3. **Develop the survey questions**. For example:

    "On a scale of 0 to 10, how likely are you to recommend our product/service to a friend or colleague?"

    This question is typically followed by an open-ended question that asks customers to explain their rating.

    "Can you please tell us why you gave this rating?"

    This allows customers to provide more detailed feedback about their experience with the product or service.

4. **Distribute the survey** to the target audience. This can be done through email, social media, or other channels.

5. **Analyze the survey results.** The NPS is calculated by subtracting the percentage of detractors from the percentage of promoters. You can also analyze the responses to the additional questions to gather more detailed insights into customer satisfaction and loyalty.

6. **Take action based on the results.** Use the insights from the survey to identify areas where you can improve the customer experience and increase customer satisfaction and loyalty. This might involve making changes to your products or services, improving customer support, or implementing other measures to improve the customer experience.

Net promoter campaigns are a fantastic tactic for local franchises like yours. You can send the survey digitally and customers can respond anonymously so they're more likely to be honest and open with their feedback.

These campaigns are not only great for figuring out your overall score, but also for identifying issues that you may not be aware of. Consider feedback like "no one returns my calls" or "I was overbilled."

If you see it once, it might've been a fluke. But, if you see that feedback time and time again, you've just identified a weakness in your company that needs attention before it damages your reputation further.

The net promoter score is considered part of the benchmarking process which is a great precursor to goal setting and strategic planning because it helps you identify areas of focus and helps you adjust your marketing, sales, and service efforts so you increase your NPS rating and grow your advocates, which ultimately leads to higher sales and profits.

In summary, NPS is a valuable tool for measuring and improving customer satisfaction and loyalty, which are key drivers of business success.

By tracking NPS over time, you can identify areas where you're performing well and areas where you need to improve and make the necessary changes to better meet the needs of your customers.

Let's put this into action. In addition to what we discussed in the last two chapters, what other KPIs are you tracking?

What evaluations can you derive from the trends?

Are you on track, off track, or exceeding your expectations?

Chapter 11: *Accelerated Growth Formula™*

If you're a seasoned owner with a thriving business, you can attest to the fact that if you don't market, you won't have a business at all.

When you do spend your time, energy, and hard-earned money on local marketing, you'll want to make sure that you get the most from your efforts.

Over the years, I developed and refined my *Accelerated Growth Formula™* to help strategically evaluate and calculate whether or not this **method of marketing** is conducive to your business. You may recognize a few of these from Chapter 12.

The four questions of the *Accelerated Growth Formula™* are:

1. **What does it cost you to reach your prospects** in your target market with a specific marketing medium over a specific period of time?

2. **What's your conversion rate percentage?** This is the number of people reached that actually turn into sales or move forward on another stage in your sales process. This can include opting into a list, scheduling a call, purchasing something, etc. You'll need to know what call-to-action you want to measure before you calculate this element.

3. **What is the gross profit on your first sale?**

   a. Calculate profit in the form of a dollar amount and gross profit as opposed to gross sales.

   b. As mentioned previously, sometimes you sell something at or below costs, also known as a loss leader, if it leads to attracting new customers or stimulates other sales.

4. **What's the long-term value of that customer?** This is measured in total sales from that customer + any referrals they produce. This is somewhat subjective and a little difficult to calculate because they may not purchase right away and occasionally, you won't know when a customer is a referral or just found you on their own. No matter the difficulty, this is still very important.

Once you've answered these questions (honestly!), you can determine if this marketing method or campaign is viable, synergistic with your other marketing, and profitable in the long run. If not, better to discover it early so you can make the necessary adjustments.

Now that you have a good idea of what you'd like to achieve and where you're starting from, we can begin looking at the additional ways to accelerate your business growth.

It's all about taking action.

1. Block out time to make a master listing of all your current local marketing methods.

2. Categorize them into traditional methods and digital marketing methods.

3. Evaluate each specific campaign using the *Accelerated Growth Formula™* to establish your baseline performance numbers. Yes, I know certain methods like outdoor signage, sponsorships, and vehicle wraps may be harder to track with the formula because those methods are designed to work synergistically with your other direct response local marketing and sales efforts.

4. Score them. Give each of your marketing methods a self-evaluated performance rating on a scale of 0 to 10, with zero being a perceived waste of money and 10 being highly effective.

5. Practice asking the four *Accelerated Growth Formula™* questions when planning any marketing campaign. Use them as an integral part of your local marketing playbook.

Chapter 12: So, You Want to Accelerate your Business

Let's face it. You're reading this book because you want to improve your business. Whether you are just starting out, struggling, or succeeding with one (or multiple) locations, you probably wouldn't say "no" to an increase in business.

But how do you achieve sustainable growth? How do you take your current state of business and improve upon it?

> *Quick reminder in case you skipped directly to this chapter.* *Check with your brand's corporate office to ensure you're operating within your best practices and approved local marketing guidelines.*

Four Methods of Growing Your Business

While every franchise business and local territory is different, there are only four basic ways that you can grow any business.

Take a look at the options below. Which of these are you focused on improving?

1. Get more **high-value customers or clients**.

2. Increase the **average transaction**.

3. Increase the **frequency of purchase or referrals**.

4. Improve your **business operational and team performance**.

Generate More High-Value Customers

Getting more customers sounds like a great idea, right? But you really don't want more customers, you want higher-value customers. Customers that have a NPS score of 9 or 10 and that actively refer new prospects to you. (NPS was explained in Chapter 11.)

Just looking for more customers becomes a curse rather than a blessing. Therefore, it's essential to focus on building relationships in your local community and delivering exceptional and frictionless customer experiences.

You can't do that if your stuck inside your business and don't block out time for local networking and outreach. This is another reason why staff training is so critical. It's hard to get new customers but super easy to lose them if your staff doesn't care about delivering quality service.

Start by evaluating who you're currently attracting through your local marketing and promotional efforts. Not all business is good business.

You'll find it a good practice to fire, or choose not to continue doing business with, the bottom 5% or 10% of your customers if they are PITAs. Pain in the Ass or not profitable. Again, focus your efforts on the higher-value customers. Notice I'm saying "value" and not "price" or "paying customers."

It's not just about the money they spend with you, it's about the relationship and ease of doing business with you. The responsibility to deliver an amazing customer experience is on you and your entire team's shoulders. Just because a customer may make a smaller purchase, or have an issue or complaint, doesn't make them a low value customer. Reasonable complaints create opportunities for excellence.

The improvement process begins with you revisiting the journey of the customer, aka the customer experience (CX), to ensure you're following your franchise brand's systems, methodologies, and best practices.

Next, take the time to sit with your key staff and discuss each step in the journey from prospect to customer to advocate. Put yourself in the mind of the prospect by considering what it looks like to do business with you. Look at everything, all touchpoints under your control.

This includes your local location's online website or store page in your brand's national directory, Google, and other review websites depending on your business model.

Do you have a Yelp, Angi, HomeAdvisor®, BBB online, MerchantCircle, OpenTable, Facebook page reviews, LinkedIn recommendations, or other review website with your local location's listing profile? Check with your head office for best practices and approved guidelines.

Dig deeper and review the quality of the communications, response times, visual appeal of your store (inside and outside), vehicles, current promotional flyers and signage, and staff appearance and training.

Think back over the last few months and make a hit list of the top issues and complaints you're getting to see if there are patterns that will help you identify areas for improvement.

Once you've done that, it's time to look at the quality of customer you're attracting and evaluate how you and your staff, particularly your salespeople or those responsible for revenue generation, are spending their time and energy.

By focusing on the higher-value prospects and converting them into new and repeat customers, you'll find that you reduce headaches, you, your team, and your customers will be happier, and you'll generate more profits.

Chapter 13: Increase the Average Transaction Value

Now that you're attracting more high-value customers, you can start to think about how to get customers to spend more money with you.

What's an average transaction for your typical customer purchase?

Do you have an idea in your head or is this variable one of your Key Performance Indicators (KPIs) that you measure monthly or by specific campaign?

Reminder: To calculate the average transaction value, you take the total sales for a given period, then divide that by the total number of sales transactions for that same period.

For example, if you sold $50,000 from 500 sales transactions in a month, then $50,000/500 = $100 average transaction for that month.

If you're a Quick Service Restaurant (QSR) franchise, like Subway®, McDonald's, Wendy's®, Freddy's Frozen Custard & Steakburgers, BeaverTails, Duck Donuts, Papa Murphy's, etc., then these numbers will be significantly different with a much greater number of transactions at smaller individual sales amounts.

Yes, your accounting software or online company portal may already track and display these important KPI numbers on an online dashboard system automatically for you. Your goal is to establish a baseline and then work to improve your average transaction. Okay, enough with the math, let's explore a few ways you can increase the average transaction.

Sure, you most likely are familiar with the methods below, but knowledge doesn't equal execution or implementation. As I've shared repeatedly, it's not what you know, but how well you execute!

The Upsell / Add-on

Upselling is a sales technique to encourage customers to spend more by buying an upgraded or premium version of what's being purchased. Going back to our Subway® example, customers who came in for a sandwich are now walking out with a sandwich, drink, and dessert. A great example of an upsell is the upsell phrase made iconic by McDonald's, "Do you want fries with that?"

Are your frontline staff people trained on how to properly offer upsell and add-on options for your products and services? Ask the customer if he or she is interested in another relevant item at the point-of-sale, during the process of taking the order via phone or in person, or through your online shopping process, especially during the checkout process.

The Cross-sell

By asking more exploratory questions related to the reasons why they (the prospects) are interested in your products and services, you are better suited for suggesting other options that can add to the initial product that they're interested in purchasing. Being prepared and training your staff to look for and identify opportunities makes it much more effective to offer a cross-sale solution. Cross-selling is very effective in converting a prospect when they decline your initial offer and you offer another suitable solution that may more closely match their budget and needs.

If you're selling through your website, you can do this automatically when someone closes a product page or abandons their shopping cart with a redirect to a cross-sale offer.

I don't want to get too technical in this book but want you to consider how you can leverage cross-selling to add more value and help your customers, while increasing your revenue too.

Create Premium / Bundle Package Offers / LTOs

Look at your list of products and services ranging from low to high and explore how you might combine a few products into a bundle package, Limited Time Offer (LTO), or other seasonal special offer. You can position this in your marketing and sales efforts by calling this a premium offer or best-value option.

Keep in mind that your customers most likely researched your local franchise and solutions to their needs and desires before they contacted you. That doesn't make them the expert, but they may feel like they are well informed.

You, the franchisee, and your team, are the expert authorities on your products and services, and creating premium or bundle offers allow you to serve your customers more fully and increases your revenue too. It's your responsibility, after you have corporate approvals, to position your solutions as the best option to serve their needs.

Remember, the customer doesn't know what they don't know, so while they may feel they are fully informed, it's your goal to show them how your offer helps solves their problems, makes their lives easier, or satisfies their needs. I encourage you to test premiums to get the most effective combination or offer.

A few years ago, I helped design and implement bundle packages for the retail locations of a pool services franchise. I was hired to be the opening keynote at their annual conference. Like all of my speaking events over the last 30 years, I mystery shopped several of their franchisees prior to the event, so I could understand their needs from the franchisee's perspective, while also becoming very familiar with their brand, customer experience, and identify opportunities for growth.

Two other factors made this pre-event research a bit easier. First, I own an in-ground pool and hot tub spa. I purchase chemicals, cleaning supplies, and monthly maintenance for my pool and spa. Second, one of my other companies sold millions worth of a children's product called *Floating Swimwear* to thousands of pool and spa dealers across the country for several years.

I exhibited at the major and regional pool and spa industry shows too, so you can imagine my excitement wanting to help independent franchisees increase their sales where many are competing against the big-box mass merchant stores.

This particular franchise brand was already very successful, but like many franchisors, they need their franchisees to follow their systems, implement best practices, and take responsibility for sales at the local level. When I visited the local franchisee location, I presented myself as a new pool and spa owner looking for chemicals and maintenance. The person behind the counter was on their phone, not paying any attention to me.

I brought a water sample for chemical testing, and they performed the test, but didn't ask me any probing questions about my needs or suggest how they could help. They did answer my questions about which type of chemicals I should use, but they could have sold me so much more.

I needed a new pool cleaner and pump, pool brush, and chemicals, just to name a few items. I left without making a purchase and went to the other location across town. Similar experience. They left hundreds of dollars on the table. Just imagine how many customers they are under serving and the massive amount of first time and repeat business they're losing.

Working with the corporate brand office, they explained to me that the average transaction sale of pool chemicals in their retail stores was approximately $85 for consumable chemical products. While the specific details of the packages

I helped them create are strictly confidential, by providing the franchisees with specific point-of-sale signage, window graphics, and most importantly, easily implemented sales strategies using bundles, their average transaction went up as much as 200% in many locations. Are bundles new? Of course not, but many times it doesn't have to be complicated to increase sales, especially when you implement upsells, cross-sells, and premium bundles.

Keeping an eye on how you can increase the average transaction value is essential, as having more money come in means there'll be more money coming out of each individual sale.

While this may seem like a challenging task, there are several steps that can be taken to help boost the amount customers spend at your store or business as covered in this chapter — from being mindful of merchandising decisions all the way through making sure customer service is top-notch.

Your numbers are starting to climb, but you still want more improvement. You find ways to bring your customers back more often and create a program where they earn rewards for referring friends.

This falls under the 3rd option for growing your business... Increasing the frequency of purchase. Simply stated... getting repeat business.

Chapter 14: Increase the Frequency of Purchases

Never before have people had this much influence on what others will buy or use, which makes customer retention and loyalty more important than ever.

A study in the *Harvard Business Review* found that increasing customer retention by 5% can lead to a whopping 25%-95% increase in revenue.

Keeping your customer relations alive will lead to repeat and referral business. It costs you way more to attract the attention of a new customer than it does to promote to customers with whom you have an existing relationship, and here are a few more recent customer loyalty statistics to prove it.

- 82% of companies agree that retention is cheaper than acquisition.

- 75% of consumers say they favor companies that offer rewards.

- 56% of customers stay loyal to brands which "get them."

- 65% of a company's business comes from existing customers.

Depending on the type of products and services you offer, especially the price points, it may not be feasible for repeat sales as much as it is for referral sales. In the case of the pool and spa franchise, purchasing a $30,000 in-ground pool hardly means I'm going to be in the business for a repeat purchase of that item anytime soon, but certainly a repeat customer for an upsell to a spa, monthly chemicals, and pool maintenance services.

Encouraging Repeat Customers

Are you tracking new vs repeat customers each month?

Acquiring new customers is important too, as you can't get repeat business if you never capture that first sale. The relationship and the likelihood of a referral or Google review is much higher for repeat customers.

Let's explore a few ways to build better relationships and encourage repeat sales using tangible and digital tactics.

- Sales and customer service training for your staff to nurture the relationship and capture new opportunities

- Limited Time Offers (LTOs) — mentioned in the previous chapter

- Thank-you package offers

- Build a community for your customers, like a Facebook group or unlisted YouTube video playlist

- Advertising specialty logo products

- Autoresponders engagement email series

- Content marketing efforts using lead magnets. Topics that provide valuable insights, product demos, or how-to guides

- Special offers for current customers, special events, early-bird access, or unique experiences

- Discounts - with caution

- Loyalty or points program

- Coupons

In summary, as a franchisee, you know that repeat customers are the key to increased sales and loyalty. The goal here is finding ways to motivate your customers to come back for additional products or services.

We discussed proven tactics such as incentivizing purchases with promotions and discounts, recognizing returning customers with rewards programs, and offering personalized services that build trusting relationships.

With these methods in your arsenal of marketing tools, you'll have all the information needed to foster long-term customer loyalty and drive consistent returns on investment!

Chapter 15: Future-Proofing Your Business: Trend & Opportunity Spotting

In the fast-paced world of business, it's important to stay ahead of the curve and anticipate future trends and opportunities. Identifying trends is important for any business, but it can be especially important for a local business. Here are a few reasons why:

Staying competitive: By identifying and adapting to trends, especially within our community, we can stay competitive and attract customers who are looking for the latest products or services.

Meeting customer needs: By staying up to date on trends, we can better understand and meet the needs of our customers. This can lead to increased customer satisfaction and loyalty.

Identifying new opportunities: Trends can open new opportunities for us to diversify our product or service offerings or to enter new markets. Again... within your brand's guidelines.

Differentiating from competitors: By being among the first to adopt and adapt to trends, we can differentiate our businesses from competitors and stand out in our local markets.

Overall, identifying trends is important for any business because it helps us stay relevant, meet customer needs, and find new opportunities for growth and success.

Let's explore various strategies for thinking ahead and identifying trends and opportunities.

Strategies for thinking ahead:

1. **Stay informed:** Make an effort to stay up to date on the latest trends and developments in your industry. This can be achieved through reading industry publications, attending conferences and events, and networking with other professionals.

2. **Monitor your competition:** Keep an eye on what your competitors are doing and look for areas where you can differentiate your business and offer something unique.

3. **Seek out new opportunities:** Look for opportunities to expand your business or develop new products and services that meet the evolving needs of your customers.

4. **Experiment and test:** Don't be afraid to try out new ideas and approaches. You can use small-scale experiments or pilot projects to test the feasibility and potential impact of new initiatives.

5. **Encourage a culture of innovation:** Foster an environment within your organization that encourages creativity and innovation. This can be achieved through regular brainstorming sessions, setting aside dedicated time for innovation, and encouraging employees to share their ideas and feedback.

6. **Keep an open mind:** Be open to new ideas and perspectives and be willing to consider different approaches to solving problems and identifying opportunities.

7. **Use data and analytics:** Leverage data and analytics to identify trends and patterns that can help you make informed decisions about the future direction of your business.

8. **Seek out expert advice:** Consider working with a business coach or consultant who can provide expert guidance and help you identify new opportunities for growth.

Having been an entrepreneur for over 40 years, I can confidently say that identifying trends is crucial for the success of any business.

By staying up to date on trends and being proactive in seeking out new opportunities, we can stay competitive, meet the needs of our customers, differentiate our businesses from our competitors, and find new avenues for growth and success.

I highly recommend that all of us make it a priority to continuously monitor trends and be on the lookout for new opportunities in our respective local markets. This proactive approach will help set us up for long-term success in an ever-changing market and economic landscape.

PART III — SKYROCKETING YOUR MARKETING RESULTS

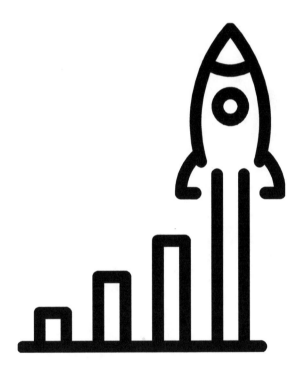

Chapter 16: Building a Referral Frenzy

Are you looking to cultivate a referral-based culture within your business? In today's hustle and bustle world, referrals have become invaluable for businesses that are seeking new customers.

Word of mouth is a powerful marketing tool; however, it can be difficult to nurture a strong referral network without the right strategies in place. With some clever techniques and an understanding of implementing these tactics effectively, building a successful system of referrals can alleviate customer acquisition stress from your plate.

Do you have a referral culture at your franchise location?

There are the typical word-of-mouth referrals and there are digital footprint referrals that come from your online reviews and social media profiles. Referrals also come from your team, vendors, and strategic partners.

Here are a few more ways to develop a referral culture in your franchise.

1. Developing a referral mindset with all your staff begins by explaining the benefits of a referral culture. It helps you:

   - Shorten the sales cycle

   - Reduce sales and marketing expenses

   - Establish trust and credibility through the referral source

   - Less price resistance because they are more confident in doing business with you

   - Loyal customers tend to multiply

   - Higher conversion rates than unqualified sales leads

2. Train your staff to say, "Thank you, don't keep us a secret." When the customer says, "What?", you say, "We're never too busy to help your friends or colleagues with **their (fill in the blank with your**

offerings) needs." This was a tip from my good friend and fellow speaker Bill Cates.

3. Refer-a-friend program rewarding customers for sending you new business.

4. Asking for the referral at the happiness moment. At the moment your customers express elation with you or your products or services is the precise time to ask for the referral.

    Just say, "Do you mind if I capture your comments on video?" and grab your cell phone to record the video. Or you can ask them to post a picture on social media and tag your business with your hashtag.

5. Send a personalized thank-you card or gift to every customer who offers a referral.

6. Send a surprise and delight package to your top customers and referral partners.

7. Add a special voice mail message on your phone system. Say something like, **"Thanks for calling _____. If you were referred to us, please let us know who we need to thank!"** This lets the prospects know you appreciate your referrals and helps build trust and credibility.

Take these steps to build a referral frenzy:

1. Review and implement the action items mentioned above.

2. Make a list of the companies in your local area that reach and sell to the same ideal client you want to reach that aren't competitors.

3. Once you have the list, reach out to them and ask them who they sell to and that you love to give referrals and that you're interested in discovering how they'd like to be introduced if you come across an ideal client for their business, products, or services. This gets the conversation started.

    Then let them know how you'd like to be introduced to their customer base. Maybe you'll offer their customers a special offer or incentive. Building your strategic referral partners is an easy way to drive lots of new business. Just make sure you align yourself with like-minded quality businesses or this strategy can backfire.

4. Provide your strategic referral partners with a special report, helpful video, or promotional materials they can share when they make a sale. Then reciprocate.

5. Train your staff using the methodology and specific language discussed in this chapter.

6. Capture video testimonials, Google reviews, and encourage referrals throughout all of your sales efforts.

Building a referral culture is one of the best forms of marketing. By encouraging your employees to refer customers and partners to your company, you can tap into a network of trusted connections that can lead to new business opportunities and increased sales.

But the benefits of a referral culture go beyond just the bottom line — it also fosters a sense of community and collaboration within your team, which can lead to increased morale and productivity. So don't underestimate the power of referrals — start building your referral culture and watch your sales take off!

In the next chapter, we're going to discuss the 3 essential elements of marketing that will unlock massive growth in your business.

Chapter 17: The Three M's Formula (3 M's) for Marketing Success

Quick Disclaimer: *Here's a quick reminder from Chapter 1: I know one of the many reasons you decided on owning a franchise brand was because the heavy lifting of branding, promotional materials, sales formulas, and quality products and services were provided to you when you got onboarded and opened your first location. This doesn't excuse you from the benefits of getting a deeper understanding of local area marketing and how to implement and execute these strategies, tactics, and formulas more effectively.*

If you've ever spent any time studying marketing, you may have been led to believe that it's this complex, incomprehensible concept that the average person can't possibly understand.

If you've ever been courted by a marketing or digital marketing company, they've likely told you that they can't guarantee their work because there are just too many aspects that come into play. Then they spouted out a whole bunch of words designed to make you feel dumb because you may not understand them, and you can't possibly implement them in your business.

None of that is true.

You're about to discover the secret weapon, the road map, the Holy Grail if you will, of marketing. It's super simple to understand... but not as easy to effectively execute. In all my years launching products and campaigns, spending my own money, and then helping hundreds of clients through my creative agency, I've identified three elements of **a marketing success formula** guaranteed to help you evaluate and improve all of your marketing and sales efforts. This is especially true for local area marketing efforts too.

Are you ready for the Three Marketing Success Formula (3 M's)?

> Connecting the right **Message (The Why) + Target Market (The Who) + Marketing Method = Success** (Greater engagement and conversions... yes, leads and sales.)

As a franchise owner, hopefully your brand's templates and marketing toolbox is already using the marketing success formula, even if they don't call it by that name.

Simple formula, right? I'm sure you understand each element to a degree.

Think of the 3 M's formula (Message, Market, Method) aspects like the digits on a combination lock. When you find the right numbers and the right combination, it unlocks your profit.

The magic of this **formula is when you get the right combination of your message, market, and method.** If what you're doing now for local marketing is working, then you've got alignment, like those proper digits in a combination lock.

If you're marketing efforts aren't yielding the results you want, I guarantee it's going to come down to one or more of those elements out of sync, and your profit potential is still locked up.

Let's take a look at each element of the 3 M's formula in greater details.

Message

The Benefits. Why should someone pay attention to you or your brand, your offer, products, or services? What's your unique value? People want to know what's in it for them, so always lead with benefits, and substantiate your claims with features.

This has also been called a Value Proposition. Make no mistake about it. Benefits are the only thing that captures attention. Benefit headlines. Benefit paragraph headings, titles of posts on social media, benefit tease intros to blogs, video titles, articles, or promotional materials.

Benefits are the results, the emotional and intangible value that the prospect experiences. If what you're saying (in any medium) is about you, your company, your product, processes, or services... it's a feature. Open 24 hours... Feature. Fast Service... Feature. Large selection... Feature. What's the result of those features? Convenience... Benefit. Saving time... Benefit. Improved shopping experience... Benefit.

Exercise: Gather up your promotional materials, look at your product or services descriptions, or print out a few pages of your website. Take two colored highlighters and highlight BENEFITS in one color and FEATURES with the other color. Some of you are going to be challenged to find any benefits... even with a search party. I'm not trying to be harsh, but the simple exercise of truly understanding the difference between benefits and features is essential to improving your marketing and sales.

Here's a few magic words to use to help convert features into benefits. Read your sales copy from any medium or promotional piece, then ask yourself, "So what?" or "Which means?"

For example, *15 years in business.* That's clearly a feature because it describes the business. Ask, "Which means?" Which means you can **trust us** and have **confidence** we can deliver. **Trust and confidence are benefits.** They are feelings and emotions. Again, lead with benefits and substantiate your claims with features.

Market

Who is your ideal customer avatar? Understanding who your target customers are is essential to marketing success. Identifying your ideal customer avatar can help you focus on strategies that will attract and motivate these types of customers into your business.

By defining your ideal customer as specifically as possible, you can craft compelling marketing messages, product offerings, and services tailored precisely to them.

So then — who is the perfect fit for what you offer? The fancy marketing terms used to define your ideal client profile, also known as avatars, are **psychographics** — behaviors and **demographics** — stats or traits.

Here are a half-dozen prompts to help you define your ideal customer avatar:

1. Define what you want your high-value targeted customer avatar to look like.

2. Describe their lifestyle, interests, and values.

3. Outline what motivates them and what challenges they face.

4. Pinpoint where they spend their time and money.

5. Determine what channels they use to gather information.

6. Create a profile that includes demographic information.

I've included downloadable Ideal Customer templates in the *ACCELERATE* Companion Tool Kit available at www.FranchiseTrainingSolutions.com/accelerate-tool-kit. Download and fill them out for each of your ideal customer categories.

Method

This is the marketing medium through which you deliver your message to the right target market. Methods fall into two main categories: 1) Traditional methods and 2) Digital methods. Each of these categories can then be broken down further into paid or low-cost or no-cost methods.

Your franchise brand uses a variety of methods. They take care of the national or global voice, and it's the local franchisee's responsibility to leverage their community knowledge and execute on local area marketing. That's been the purpose of this entire book.

Disclaimer number... anyway

This is important. I absolutely recognize and agree that you, as a franchise owner, may rely heavily on your national corporate brand (ZOR) to provide you with pre-designed, and hopefully proven, promotional materials, templates, and best practices.

That said, it's still up to you to execute and use them wisely to reach your local community prospects and customer. The 3 M's formula works. Master it. I'm here for you. Let me know if you have any questions.

Exercise 1:

Create a list of your marketing methods (both traditional and digital) that you're responsible for at the local level as a ZEE. I've added a few items to get you started.

1. **Print advertising** in local newspapers and community magazines.

2. **Direct mail** marketing.

3. **Cold calling** and telemarketing.

4. **Outdoor advertising,** such as billboards and signage.

5. Local **sponsorship** and **partnerships**.

6. **Networking** and attending local events and **trade or consumer shows**.

7. Creating and **distributing flyers** and other promotional materials.

8. **Word-of-mouth** marketing and referrals from satisfied customers.

9. Offering **discounts** and **special promotions** to local customers.

10. Providing **excellent customer service** to encourage repeat business and **positive reviews**.

11. Using **coupons** and other promotional offers in local newspapers and other print media.

12. Offering **loyalty programs** and **rewards to repeat customers**.

13. Collaborating with other local businesses on **joint marketing** efforts and **cross-promotions**.

14. Advertising on local **radio and television** stations.

15. Creating a strong presence on **local online directories** and **review websites**.

16. Posting local, timely, and topical content on your **local location's website** page and **social media** profiles. (Make a specific list of each social media site that you maintain as a ZEE.)

17. Using **email marketing** to reach out to local customers and subscribers.

18. Offering **in-store demonstrations** and **product samples** to attract new customers.

19. Participating in or presenting at **community events** to network and raise awareness for your business.

20. Creating **engaging and informative content**, such as blog posts, videos, podcasts, and infographics, to attract local customers.

21. **What others do you use?** Or a better question, are you now going to use because of your renewed excitement about local area marketing?

Exercise 2:

BENCHMARK: Before you spend another dollar on paid advertising, producing new promotional materials, or integrated marketing campaigns (see Chapter 21), please utilize the 3 M's Marketing Success Formula to help you establish a benchmark performance rating on a scale of 1 to 100, yes, 100 this time means that your combination of the 3 M's is extremely successful.

> **Here's the 3 M's formula again as a refresher:**
>
> Connecting the right **Message (The Why) + Target Market (The Who) + Marketing Method = Successful conversions and higher sales**.

If you're not getting the performance you desire or expect from a marketing campaign, adjust one or more of the elements, and then test again.

Test small first, then once you're happy with the conversion rates and performance, expand your investment.

The key is to start your test conservatively, then get more complicated and aim to beat the performance of your control campaign.

Chapter 18: Three M's Formula Case Studies

Are you ready for an epic fail when the 3 M's formula isn't used?

Comcast® Spectator Case Study #1

Back in 1994, before the internet was really a thing, and before many of you reading this book where even born…, I was hired to present on *Innovative Marketing Mastery* for a division of Comcast®, the telecommunications giant.

The outcome of the event was to help them improve their marketing and sales of their large sports and entertainment centers. We'd accomplish that goal through a combination of innovative exercises, marketing formulas, and interactive hot seat marketing critiques.

The event brought together their general managers and senior marketing executives, marketing, and salespeople who helped manage large venues, arenas, and sports complexes across the United States.

These were the people responsible for ticket sales, you know butts in seats, for sporting events like baseball and hockey, music concerts, Ice Capades, circuses, Sesame Street Live!, and any other monstrous event you can imagine.

It's safe to say that every person in that room was making over $100k a year, some double that. The math on that salary equivalence today is over a million dollars. These were talented and savvy professionals. I was hired by the Vice President of Marketing of that division who wanted me to share trends and innovative ways they could increase their marketing and sales performance.

I was a bit intimidated, since my speaking business was only a couple of years old at that time and this was a big client. It's also safe to say that no one really was too excited to sit in a workshop all day when they were having the event at a luxury golf resort.

Secretly, and some not so secretly, felt like they already knew everything and would rather be playing golf. Not because of me, they hadn't heard one word out of my mouth yet.

As I was being introduced by the VP for my presentation, many of the attendees weren't in their seats yet. They were still huddled around the breakfast buffet or reading the newspaper. There weren't any smartphones back then or I'm sure they all would have been glued to their smartphones for email or watching TikTok videos.

As the introduction was completed, the VP walked off the stage leaving the group to me. Now what do I do? Half the room wasn't sitting, and the half that was wasn't even paying attention to my introduction. Sweat started running down my forehead, I felt dizzy, and I was close to having a panic attack.

Being the shy little flower I am, I raised my voice and sent a booming noise over the audio speaker system.

"Hey! Good morning, everyone," ... and waited for the room to become silent. I then said, "Please give me 15 minutes of your time. If you don't like what I'm talking about or find it valuable, you can leave and go play golf. How's that sound? It really doesn't matter to me... I've already got my check."

Yes. I said that in a moment of fear. My inner voice became my outer voice. Oops, that's a mistake I'll never have on stage again. Okay, back to the true story...

I could feel the VP shooting daggers and could sense the shockwave through the room as people took their seats.

"Thank you," I said. "Now, who in this room is considered to be one of your top producers? Who's a marketing rock star? Please join me on stage and bring your samples of your advertising and promotional materials with you."

You see, I was supposed to deliver about 45 minutes of value-added insights and content before the 45 minutes of interactive hot seat critiques, but I was trying to avoid a train wreck.

A man jumped to his feet, all proud, and said, "I'm considered a rock star... give me your best shot, kid," and he joined me at the front of the room. We'll call him Steve. The story is true, but I've changed his name for confidentiality. "Thanks for coming up, Steve. Can you show me some marketing pieces that you're really proud of?"

He shuffled through his stack of marketing samples and handed me a section of newspaper that had a full-page advertisement for Sesame Street Live! playing in the venues he managed. Side note. Newspapers were still a somewhat viable promotional method back in 1994.

I started with my 3 M's formula.

"So, Steve," I said, "let's take a look and see what we can find in the way of a benefit headline and compelling sales narrative (message) and evaluate whether or not that message is targeted at your ideal customer avatars (market), and see if the medium you're using, the newspaper full-page advertisement (medium), is unlocking engagement and helping increase ticket sales. How does that sound to you, Steve?" "That sounds great," he said, with his gloating confident smirk beginning to wane a bit.

My first question was, "How much did you spend on the full-page ads?" (Remember this question as part of the *Accelerated Growth Formula*™ we discussed back in Chapter 13?)

He said that it was over $50,000, and he had signed a monthly insertion order contract media buy for six months. He was committed to six months to lock in better pricing for the frequency of contracting ad space. This meant his METHOD variable was set for months, but he could change the advertisements with enough lead time for printing.

Let's see if I can describe and paint a visual mental picture of the full-page advertisement in the biggest local newspaper.

Imagine a full-page display add with a large picture of Big Bird, one of the Sesame Street cartoon characters, along with the headline, "Let's Be Friends!", and then below Big Bird was a details box with the dates and times of upcoming shows, with pricing and parking details and a simple call-to-action (CTA) to call or come to the box office to get tickets.

I asked him who the headline, "Let's Be Friends!" and the display ad was designed for, and he said, "Kids, of course!"

My next question was to ask who was the ideal customer for Sesame Street shows? And Steve said, "Well, families with small kids," his voice a bit less confident.

"And what section of the newspaper did you run this ad in?" Holding it up high for the entire audience to see. Steve was now silent, and you could have heard a pin drop. All eyes were on me holding up this full-page display ad he had printed in the financial section of the paper.

"Remind me again how much you paid for this ad, Steve?"

He straightened up even more in his seat on stage and proudly proclaimed, "$50,000. In fact, I got 20% off because they used remnant space and a six-month deal."

"So let me get this straight, Steve," I said clearly into my microphone. "You spent $50,000 to send the message 'Let's Be Friends!' to small children who are supposed to see and read this in the financial section of the newspaper?" Now Steve was the one starting to sweat.

I continued, "So you're the rock star top producer, yet you're sending the headline and design of the advertisement, without any benefit copy or sales narrative, to the wrong avatar." Epic fail.

"I understand that you've already paid for the ad space, and I don't want you to lose those marketing dollars… but I also don't know many children who read the newspaper," I said. "So, what if we rebuilt this advertisement using the 3 M's formula? What if we focused on the parents as the market and attracted attention with a more relevant image and benefit narrative for attending Sesame Street Live!?"

The audience was paying full attention now.

"Let's remove Big Bird, add a lifestyle picture with a happy family smiling and enjoying each other's company wearing swag from the event, and add benefit copy that speaks to how Sesame Street Live! creates a lifetime of memories and provides quality family time."

We spent the 90 minutes reviewing and improving the rest of their marketing materials using the 3 M's marketing success formula. Fast forward. After the event and their teams started implementing the 3 M's formula, sales conversions increased, and Comcast® hired me multiple times for consulting and training for several of their other divisions.

Everyone loves to save money. But if your message, market, and method don't work together, you're just a big yellow bird in a sea of stock numbers.

Let's look at a few other examples of how the right 3 M's can make all the difference.

Bicycle Storage Solutions Case Study #2

I've always been an entrepreneur. From my early days in the painting business to my current businesses, Prime Concepts and Franchise Training Solutions, I've always looked for the problems that I could solve. But I didn't always have a strong grasp of the 3 M's formula.

In 1984, I was a professional Cat 3 cyclist. In perspective, Lance Armstrong was a Cat 1 Pro. I had two $10k bikes at the time (and that's $10k in 1984 numbers) and nowhere to put them. I was living in an apartment at the time, and I sure as hell wasn't going to leave the bikes outside to be stolen or subjected to the elements.

As I sat there staring at my already-cramped apartment, I knew there had to be a better way to store these bicycles. The short story is that I invented, designed, patented, manufactured, and then promoted a complete line of bicycle storage solutions. These were unique, floor-to-ceiling oak and aluminum stands that held up to four bikes, without having to drill holes into the walls or ceiling. I briefly mentioned this in an earlier chapter.

After all, what good was it if I lost my security deposit?

I decided that my message was to protect your bicycles without damaging your walls or ceilings. My market was anyone else who owned bikes, especially cyclists with expensive bikes that didn't want to leave them outside to be ruined or stolen or junk up their garage or apartment. Finally, my method was to exhibit at local and national bicycle races and sell directly to consumers. Retail direct.

During the first 6 months, I drove across the country from race to race. I would stand in my little 10x10 tented booth for hours explaining my product and taking a handful of orders at each event. This process was high-labor intensive, extremely time consuming, and honestly, it didn't make very much in gross sales and very little net profit.

I knew I was doing something wrong. This was before I knew anything formal about marketing formulas. I thought my market was bike racers, and while they purchased and ultimately benefited from my product, they were the wrong market because they didn't want to spend $200 on an oak bike rack, they'd rather invest it in new bicycle gear or on getting to races. Epic fail.

Fast forward, my product didn't change, I just corrected my 3 M's. And I generated millions in gross sales. I changed my retail marketing messages and aimed them at females and homeowners, along with wholesale marketing messages aimed at bicycle shops, specialty mail order catalogs, mass merchant retailers, chain stores, and companies that specialize in organizing garages and small spaces.

I turned a 5-figure business into a mid-7-figure business in only a few short years. That's when I refined the 3 M's formula because I was selling through so many different channels of distribution and a global marketplace.

Floating Swimwear for Kids and Adults Case Study #3

What does a 26-year-old kid do when they start to make more money? Invest it. That would have been smart, but I decided to buy a boat. So, I did. It was a 27' Bayliner boat that slept four and even had a small shower and toilet.

I was becoming a successful entrepreneur; it was time to enjoy it. I'd dreamed of owning a cabin cruiser boat at our local lake for years. I imagined myself spending my weekends away from the office surrounded by my wife and our adorable small son. We'd have the wind in our hair, all of our cares just disappearing into the open water.

Of course, that was the dream. The reality looked a lot different.

My wife was terrified that our son, Logan, age 5 going on 15, would fall off the boat and drown. Let me set the stage. The lake was less than a mile wide and only 20 or 30 ft deep, very calm waters, and hardly qualified as a big lake. It was big enough for a boat, but you could never get lost because you could always see the shoreline.

The only way she'd let him out on the water was wearing one of those orange horse collar uncomfortable life jackets. Poor little Logan, he was miserable because in addition to the life jacket, my wife tied a short rope to him, like a dog on a leash. My wife was always worried he would fall off the boat, so she fluttered around him like a helicopter. This wasn't how I imagined the weekend getaways with the picture in my head.

Then one summer, I went to a local consumer boat show. Those of you that have a boat understand that if you have a boat, you're always looking for new gadgets or spending money maintaining your boat.

Walking up and down the show aisles, a banner caught my eye. FLOATING SWIMWEAR, Keep your Kids Safe in and Around Water. I could barely contain my excitement. The product was a Lycra swimsuit with soft flotation material sewn into it. I imagined how happy Logan would be in what looked like a superhero costume. I knew Logan would love it, and maybe my wife would relax a bit or even be happy. And ultimately, we all could finally enjoy the boating experience.

I walked up to the booth and said, "I'll take 2 please."

"Don't you want to know how much it costs?" said the man working the booth. Now I'm sure he meant well, but he certainly wasn't trained to recognize buying signals. Did I care about the price or was I thinking about the emotional benefits of reducing pain and increasing pleasure? Pleasure of course.

"That's a silly question, just ring me up for a couple suits, thank you," I said. "Here's my credit card." I grabbed the bag and my receipt for $70 (2 x $35 ea.) and walked about 10 steps away, then turned and reapproached his booth.

I introduced myself and gave him my business card. I took a couple minutes explaining I had a successful sporting goods manufacturing and distribution company, and I could really help him scale his business.

"This is a great product," I told him. "I'd love to help you dramatically expand your distribution and increase your sales."

The owner laughed at me as if I was crazy and said, "Kid, if I had a nickel for everyone who told me I'd make millions, I would have retired long ago."

When I got to the marina and Logan put on the floating swimwear suit, the other boaters and people on the docks couldn't stop staring. Everyone wanted to know what it was and where they could get suits for their kids. After just a few minutes, I was approached by so many people that I left the boat tied to the marina and rushed back to the boat show.

Take #2 at the booth. "I want to buy your inventory, give me everything you have, and I'll load it up right now." The owner lifted an eyebrow and began to shake his head. "I can't. I have to be here for three days."

This guy was killing me.

I finally convinced him to listen to reason, and I negotiated a deal. I filled my van up with over a hundred units, and I drove back to the marina. I made a deal with the marina manager to remove the potato chips from the shelf near the cash register.

This was a high traffic impulse purchase area. We made a sign with a Sharpie and placed a few of the Floating Swimwear Suits there instead. We sold them for $50 each and sold out of all the inventory in just two weeks.

The owner called me a few days later to see how badly I'd failed. "So, what did you do with three years of inventory?"

"I sold it all within two weeks." I had his attention now.

Fast forward, he hired me for $25k to create a business and strategic marketing plan. Using the 3 M's formula, we changed all of his 3 M's. Changed the sales model (METHOD) and exhibited at wholesale B2B Trade Shows. Changed the marketing (MESSAGE) to aim at pool and spa dealers (MARKET) promoting, "an instant profit center for your pool and spa store."

He then became a retainer client, and we grew his little garage operation from 5 figures to over 10 million in sales in only a few short years. Let me tell you. The 3 M's Marketing Success Formula works.

Your products and services are important, but how you market consistently is even more important.

Keep the 3 M's in mind when creating or executing any marketing or sales promotion, and you'll unlock amazing leads and sales.

Chapter 19: Demystifying Traffic and Lead Generation

There are literally hundreds of marketing choices, strategies, methodologies, and tactics to choose from to help you create awareness, increase interest, improve engagement, capture leads, and activate sales.

Disclaimer in case you've jumped ahead to this chapter. *Please follow your brand's systems, guidelines, approval processes, and utilize your preferred services providers.*

How many of these do you desire for your business?

We Want: (Please check all that apply.)

- ❑ More demand for our products or services

- ❑ The phone to ring with more hot leads

- ❑ More customers through the door or drive-through windows

- ❑ Targeted visitors to our website (or branded location page on the national website)

- ❑ More opt-in subscribers to our email lists

- ❑ Higher conversion rates from our advertising and promotional efforts

- ❑ More referrals

- ❑ To shorten our sales cycle

- ❑ To put our marketing on autopilot that keeps our sales pipeline full

- ❑ To increase our average sale and long-term value of a customer

- ❑ More engagement from our social media marketing efforts

- ❑ An ever-growing number of 5-star Google reviews

- ❑ To turn our customers into advocates with a NPS score above 8

- ❑ To attract, retain, and engage our staff

- ❑ Reduce the cost to acquire a customer

- ❑ We could go on for days and days with this list.

Bottom line. Regardless of our revenue model... B2B or B2C, as business owners or operators, we all want more traffic and leads, and ultimately high sales volume at greater profits. So, let's focus on driving traffic and lead generation.

For this discussion, traffic generation is getting your prospects to move from suspects >> to prospects >> to qualified prospects >> to leads that are interested in your products or services. Your "crawl over broken glass, mouthwatering, got to have it, value-added" solutions.

Keep in mind that our ultimate goal is to reach more targeted prospects and get them to take the action step you want them to take. I love to take complicated and confusing topics, demystify them, and make them easier to understand concepts. Let's do that now.

Here are the TOP 3 Ways to Generate Traffic:

1. You create it. (Content marketing)

You create it, with "it" being traffic, by sharing value-added, informational, educational, and engaging content in a variety of formats (text, email, audio, print, and video), through traditional or digital mediums, to the prospects in your community.

How? First, you'll want to make sure that digital footprint (website, SEO, social media profiles,) and physical retail location is fresh, clean, and updated with easy to lead capture processes and clear calls-to-action.

Then, you'll create bait (in the form of content, also known as lead magnets).

Lead magnets are incentives that you can offer to potential customers in exchange for their contact information, such as their email or mailing address.

These can be effective for attracting new customers because they provide value to the customer and can help to build trust and credibility for your business.

Some examples of lead magnets include e-books, white papers, webinars, and free trials. To create a lead magnet, you'll want to first identify what your target audience is interested in and what problems they are looking to solve. Then, create a piece of content that addresses those needs and offers a solution. Make sure to include a clear call-to-action that encourages the customer to provide their contact information in order to receive the lead magnet. Additionally, consider offering a limited-time discount or special offer to incentivize customers to take action.

Your lead magnets become the bait in the water. The water being in front of where your target prospects congregate online and offline. They see the bait, nibble, and hopefully bite, and you capture the lead.

Then it's up to your salespeople or sales process to move them through your sales pipeline to purchase. You share those lead magnets as companion pieces integrated with all of your marketing methods and at appropriate places in your sales process.

Here's a Few of My Lead Magnet Examples:

- Get a complimentary **Digital Marketing Critique** to improve your traffic generation, just visit PrimeConcepts.com. There are promo links at the top and bottom of the website.

- If you want to pick my brain, visit www.15withFord.com and grab a slot on my calendar.

Get your copy of my research white paper and trend report on *Employment Strategies to Drive Business Growth* at ProfitRichResults.com/employment-strategies-report.

- Watch this short explainer video on *Capturing Prospects Using Lead Magnets*. Visit FranchiseTrainingSolutions.com/accelerate-tool-kit.

I've shared additional links to bonus materials and QR codes throughout this book. All examples above are traffic generation and lead magnet strategies.

Why do savvy authors provide bonus materials and companion resources? Because if you get this book as a gift for attending a corporate meeting or purchase it on Amazon, I don't know who you are, and you're not on my customer list, you're a customer of Amazon or your favorite bookseller. I want to grow my list, so I can share my next book title when it's released. Relax, I'm not going to send you a bunch of spam. Okay, let's continue.

2. You borrow it. (Leverage other people's influence)

Borrowing someone else's influence that already has a strong following, big list, or group that reaches the same ideal customer that you want to reach. Not competitors, but maybe vendors, referral partners, influencers, local television channels, radio stations, podcasts, news outlets, or local association chapter meetings. A fancy term for this traffic generation category is called Fusion Marketing.

Fusion marketing involves the cooperation between two non-competitive businesses with a target audience and values that aim at achieving the strategic goals with a minimum, and in some cases, zero cost.

Some things will make you smarter, but not make you more money. Do you feel smarter now? *Sorry, it's 2 am, and I'm trying to finish this revised and updated manuscript and am leaving in this little Easter egg to see if you're paying attention. Ping me on LinkedIn with the magic words, "Fusion Marketing" as proof of life.*

My guess is that you've seen hundreds of examples of fusion marketing in the past, but maybe didn't know what the fancy term was until today.

Here's a popular example of how a couple of big brands use fusion marketing. Consider the Star Wars toys in McDonald's Happy Meals. Both companies benefit from working together.

On a smaller scale, you could partner with other vendors or stores that cater to your target prospects and exchange specials flyers, Limited Time Offers (LTOs), Point-of-Purchase (POP) stands, business card stacks, or offer each other's customers discounts on non-competing services.

Fusion marketing helped me accelerate my line of bicycle storage solutions when I struck a deal to add a discount coupon card in the boxes of Bell bicycle helmets, and I put Bell helmet brochures in the boxes of my products.

Let me tell you, I got the better end of that deal. Bell helmets sold millions of helmets reaching far more customers, much faster, with my brochures in their boxes than any of the other marketing promotions at that time. I was selling a few thousand units a month. They sold thousands of units per week.

If you're a franchise founder or C-level executive and you'd like to be featured on my FORDIFY LIVE broadcast (we go LIVE weekly on multiple platforms) and tell the story of your brand, just email or call me. My contact info is in the resources section at the back of your book. Why would you do this? Because it will help you elevate your brand in the eyes of other franchise owners and drive leads. As you know, many franchisees own multiple franchises with different brands.

3. You buy it. (Paid advertising)

Yep. This one is as simple as the paragraph title. You pay to send your marketing messages to your target prospects. Also known as paid advertising.

This includes all forms of advertising, traditional and digital, direct mail, display ad campaigns, and pay-per-click (PPC) just to name a few. You get it. Let's continue.

No matter what type of marketing you decide to engage in, keep in mind that all marketing is, is a way to reach, connect, educate, and build relationships with your potential customers.

Chapter 20: TABOO TOPICS — Proceed with Caution

CAUTION: MANAGED BY CORPORATE HEADQUARTERS OR PREFERRED VENDORS

A hot topic that always comes up during my pre-event speaking meeting with franchise executives is where is the line drawn for responsibilities when it comes to digital marketing and websites?

The answer I get is the main website is managed by the ZOR, but the ZEE has a page or section with an admin panel they can use to enhance with a local flare, pictures, and messaging, but the rest of the page elements, headers, footers, colors, navigation, are maintained by the ZOR or a preferred authorized services provider.

Brand Consistency

Most franchise brands may prevent local franchisees from having their own websites or social media accounts for several reasons. One of the main reasons is to maintain consistency and control over the brand's online presence.

By having a centralized online presence, the franchise can ensure that all of its locations are presenting the brand in a consistent manner, and that the information that is being presented is accurate.

Avoid Confusion Among Customers

Another reason why franchise brands may prevent local franchisees from having their own websites or social media accounts is to avoid confusion among customers. By having a centralized online presence, customers always have access to the most accurate and up-to-date information about the brand.

Managing the Online Reputation of the Brand

Additionally, having a centralized online presence can make it easier for the franchise to monitor and manage its online reputation.

By having control over the brand's online presence, the franchise can more easily respond to customer inquiries, complaints, and reviews, and can take steps to address any issues that may arise.

That said, most brands do want the franchisee to monitor local complaints and help grow positive reviews.

One the next page is a list of the main topics that have purposely been limited or omitted in this book because they may easily cause friction with the ZEE and ZOR relationship.

Consult your brand's policies, training guidelines, follow your systems, and everybody wins big!

Review the list and mark the appropriate column and make notes for each method.

MARKETING METHOD	Managed on a NATIONAL LEVEL	Optional using a PREFERRED VENDOR	Managed at the FRANCHISEE LEVEL
Your Local Website Page on the National Website			
Search Engine Optimization (SEO)			
Pay-Per-Click Advertising Campaigns			
My Google Business Local Listings			
Online Reputation Services			
Social Media Marketing (by platform)			
SMS and Text Back Marketing			
Email Marketing Services			
Others?			

Want more? I'm happy to provide insights and answers to the above topics. Visit www.15withFord.com.

Remember, *ACCELERATE* is filled with easy to glean valuable insights, strategies, and tactics, I just know that many brands prefer to provide their own guidelines. Thank you for your understanding.

Chapter 21: The Importance of Integrated Marketing in the Digital Age

An integrated approach allows you to coordinate your local marketing campaigns and ensure consistent messaging throughout multiple channels of communication — from traditional media, like print ads and radio spots, all the way through digital platforms such as social media and email marketing.

Integrated marketing can be particularly effective for local franchises, as it allows you to align your marketing efforts with the overall brand while also tailoring your messages and promotions to the specific needs and preferences of your local customers in your community.

Marketing has become ever more complicated in some ways, and much easier in others. One fundamental truth is that all marketing methods, physical and digital categories, are synergistically intertwined if you want to be successful.

What's the **one common denominator with your ideal customers**? I'd say that over 99% if not 100% of them have **internet access and are influenced by what they see online**.

This has forced savvy marketers and brands of all sizes to leverage the power of integrated marketing, with the ZOR handling the national level and the ZEE responsible for traditional, grassroots, and local digital marketing within the brand's guidelines.

Integrated marketing examples:

- A local pizza franchise creates a social media campaign on their approved local Facebook page that promotes a new menu item and also includes a discount code for customers to use when ordering online or in-store. The discount code is also included in the franchise's email newsletter and on flyers that are distributed in the local community.

- A local gym franchise runs a television ad that showcases its new fitness classes and facilities and includes a call-to-action to follow the local gym on social media for more information and local updates. The gym's social media channels then feature posts that highlight individual classes and trainers and offer special promotions to community followers.

- A local nail salon franchise creates a series of videos that demonstrate how to use their nail care products at home and shares these videos on their location's website page, local social media channels, and email newsletter. The salon also includes their information about the products and where to purchase them in their print advertising.

By coordinating their marketing efforts across multiple channels, these local franchises can effectively promote their brand and products to their target audience, while also providing a consistent and high-quality customer experience.

Integrated Marketing Works

When done well, an integrated marketing approach seamlessly ties together multiple advertising avenues to yield a higher return on investment than any single channel could provide alone.

By the very nature of owning a local franchise, you're participating in integrated marketing because there are marketing efforts designed for a consistent national brand voice on a national level which, combined with your LAM efforts, drives leads and sales for your location.

Chapter 22: Social Media Networking... or Not Working?

Disclaimer #672 *Don't post anything on social media about your franchise brand, products, services or customers without reviewing your brand's guidelines or getting approvals and reread Chapter 20 "TABOO TOPICS."*

They're Just Databases

All social media websites are really just databases. The platforms evolve constantly, but once you realize they are just databases where you can have a profile, post and search content, and communicate in communities, they become less intimidating.

Ultimately, they are communication channels that offer many opportunities... but they also come with risks and online reputation challenges.

Different approaches for ZORs vs ZEEs

A local franchisee and a national franchisor may use social media marketing in similar ways, but there may be significant differences in their approach. Both may use social media to promote their products or services, engage with customers, and build brand awareness.

A local franchisee (ZEE) is likely to focus their social media efforts on the specific location or locations in a designated territory. This may involve promoting any special offers or events that are happening at their location, as well as highlighting the unique aspects of their franchise. They may also use their locally managed social media profiles to connect with local customers and address any questions or concerns they may have, again, on a local level. (See disclaimer above.)

On the other hand, a national franchisor (ZOR) may use social media to promote the overall brand and its values. They may also use social media to share information about the franchise as a whole, including any new products or services that are available. In addition, a national franchisor may use social media to communicate with all of their franchisees and provide them with support and resources.

Just because you can, doesn't mean you should

There are several reasons why a local franchise may **NOT** want (or approve you) to use social media as part of a marketing strategy, including, but not limited to:

1. **Lack of time or resources:** Managing a social media presence can be time-consuming and require dedicated resources, such as staff members who are trained in social media marketing. For a small local franchise, this may not be feasible.

2. **Limited audience:** Depending on the location of the franchise and the type of business it is, the audience for the franchise's social media channels may be relatively small. This could make it difficult to justify the time and effort required to maintain a social media presence.

3. **Potential for negative feedback:** Social media allows customers to share their experiences, both positive and negative, with a wide audience. For a local franchise, this could be a double-edged sword, as a single negative review or comment on social media, especially if left unnoticed, could have a significant negative impact on the franchise's reputation. And I'm sure you've seen a few epic fails, especially on TikTok and YouTube.

4. **Difficulty standing out:** With so many businesses using social media, it can be difficult for a local franchise to stand out and attract attention on these platforms. This can make it difficult to effectively reach potential customers and generate leads, unless you're willing to boost posts, advertise, and pay to play.

Overall, while social media can be a valuable marketing tool, it may not be the right choice for every local franchise. It's important for businesses to carefully evaluate the potential benefits and drawbacks of using social media before making a decision or giving access to untrained staff members to manage it for you.

Chapter 23: Video Marketing: Because Reading is Hard

A word is a word. A picture is worth 1000 words. A video is worth at least a 10X impact.

Disclaimer #368 *Gotta say it again in case you jumped ahead to this chapter. Please follow your brand's approved guidelines and best practices before posting any videos or social media posts to your local social media profiles. Okay, let's continue.*

Why Video?

It's easy to see why video has become such a popular choice for businesses and individuals alike. In today's fast-paced, visually driven world, video has proven to be a highly effective way to engage and inform audiences.

Here are a few reasons why video has become a preferred medium over reading text:

1. **Videos are easy to consume:** People are more likely to watch a video than read an article or blog post, especially if the video is well-produced and engaging. This is especially true on social media, where videos often receive higher engagement rates than other types of content.

2. **Videos are more memorable:** Research has shown that people are more likely to remember information presented in a video than in text form. This is because videos combine auditory and visual stimuli, which can help to reinforce the message and make it more memorable.

3. **Videos can convey emotion and personality:** Text can only convey so much, but video allows you to showcase your brand's personality and values through body language, tone of voice, and visual elements. This can help to build a stronger connection with your audience and make your message more impactful.

4. **Videos are versatile:** Video can be used in a variety of contexts and formats, from short social media clips to longer-form explainer videos

or webinars. This makes it a versatile and flexible medium for any type of business or message.

Overall, video is a powerful and popular medium that can help us to effectively engage and inform our prospects and customers on a local level.

Using videos for marketing, sales, customer service, and even operations just makes common sense, but is this common practice for you?

Most social media is all video, live video, video shorts, and long form. Our smartphones have 4K cameras and easy-to-use apps. It's super simple to take, edit, and publish videos to expand awareness, attract a following, and improve your local marketing efforts.

By using short videos, because people have the attention span of a gnat. Squirrel... we can showcase our products or services, introduce our team, and provide an inside look at our local business.

This can help to build trust and establish a connection with potential customers, which can ultimately lead to increased sales and revenue. Videos can also help to improve search engine optimization (SEO) by providing more content for search engines to index, which can help to improve your business's visibility on the web.

Additionally, videos can be shared on social media or used in conjunction with email marketing or within your sales funnels, which can help to increase a business's reach and attract new customers.

Video is an important tool for local area marketing. What's your favorite video platform? Better question, what do you think are the best platforms you can utilize to get in front of your target prospects?

Here are 10 ideas to get you started:

1. Use videos to **showcase** your business's products or services.

2. Create **behind-the-scenes** videos to give customers a look at your business operations.

3. Create customer **testimonial** videos to showcase satisfied customers.

4. Use videos to announce sales or **promotions**.

5. Create **instructional or tutorial** videos to demonstrate your products or services.

6. Create video content for **social media** to engage with your audience.

7. Use videos in **email marketing** to increase click-through rates.

8. Create **live videos** to connect with customers in real-time.

9. Use videos for **local SEO** to improve your business's online visibility.

10. Create videos to **tell your business's story** and connect with customers on a personal level.

Avoid these common mistakes when creating your videos.

1. **Not having a clear objective:** Before starting to create a video, it's important to have a clear idea of what you want to accomplish with it. This will help you create a video that is focused and effective.

2. **Lack of planning:** Creating a video without a plan can result in a disorganized and unprofessional final product. Take the time to plan out your video, including the script, visuals, and any special effects or animations you want to include.

3. **Poor lighting and sound:** Poor lighting and sound can make a video difficult to watch and can distract from the content. Make sure to use good lighting and sound equipment to ensure that your video is clear and easy to understand.

4. **Not engaging the audience:** A video that doesn't engage the audience is likely to be quickly forgotten. Make sure to include elements that will grab the audience's attention, such as humor, storytelling, or interactive elements.

5. **Not optimizing for different platforms:** Different platforms have different requirements for video content, so it's important to optimize your video for the specific platform you plan to use. For example, videos on social media should be short and attention-grabbing, while videos on your website can be longer and more in-depth.

This is a great time for you to take a break and watch these two short episodes of FORDIFY. You can find them at:
www.FranchiseTrainingSolutions.com/accelerate-tool-kit.

- *How to Create Compelling Videos:* bit.ly/fords-video-tips

- *YouTube Optimization Basics:* bit.ly/fordsyoutubetips

Chapter 24: Building Community Connections: The Power of Local Networking

You've heard it before… but this LAM tactic is worth hearing again. It's that important, but before you tell me you can't because you're too busy or wearing too many hats, let me ask you a couple questions.

Are you too busy to create a foundation of sales opportunities to help you scale your business?

Are you too busy to reduce your recruiting costs to find quality candidates to work for you?

I hope not. Networking is an investment, not an expense. And if you're struggling with time management, please reread Chapters 7 and 8 with ways to reclaim your time, so you'll have time to attend local events.

Still not convinced? Local networking can help you by:

1. **Building relationships:** Local networking allows you to build relationships with other local business owners, community leaders, and potential customers. This can help you gain valuable insights into the local market and identify opportunities for growth.

2. **Increasing brand awareness:** Networking with local organizations and events can help increase brand awareness for your franchise. This can lead to more foot traffic and sales, as well as positive word-of-mouth marketing.

3. **Gaining access to resources and support:** Local networking can provide you with access to resources and support that can help you grow your franchise. This may include access to funding, partnerships, and mentorship opportunities.

4. **Providing opportunities for collaboration:** Local networking can provide opportunities for collaboration with other local businesses. This can lead to mutually beneficial relationships and help both businesses grow.

So, if you're not already networking in your community, last week was the time to start!

Here's a dozen ways to find local networking opportunities. Pick the ones that are most relevant to your business:

1. Join a local **chamber of commerce** or **business association**. This will allow you to network with other local businesses and learn about upcoming events and opportunities.

2. Attend local networking events, such as **business mixers and conferences**. These events are specifically designed to help businesses connect and make new contacts. If you don't want to commit to an organization, there are always lots of other individual events where you can meet people. You can find these through Facebook Events, Google (search "Local Business Networking Near Me"), nonprofit events, Eventbrite, your local chamber of commerce (as mentioned above), and your local convention and visitors bureau.

3. Participate in **community events** and organizations. This can help you get to know other local businesses and build relationships with potential clients and partners.

4. Join a **networking group**. Many cities and towns have networking groups that meet on a regular basis to share referrals and discuss business-related topics. Look for established social gatherings like Lions Club, Rotary, Toastmasters, Kiwanis, etc. While these may not be intended strictly for networking, they allow you to build relationships and expand your network.

5. **Networking Organizations** like BNI (Business Networking International) are designed specifically to build business relationships and generate referrals. You'll be asked to "train" your fellow members to know when and how to refer you.

   For example, if you own a gym franchise, you may ask the other members to listen out for "I need to get into shape" or "I have no energy" in their daily conversations. When they hear that, they'll know how to mention your business and pass along a referral. Each week (or however frequently your meetings are) you'll be asked to make a request of what (or who) you're looking for to improve your business.

6. **Connect virtually** with other businesses on social media. This can be a great way to find out about local networking opportunities and to

get to know other businesses in your area. Think beyond just your target customers, but about what other businesses reach the same ideal customers because they can be great sources of referrals too, like we discussed in Chapter 16, on "Creating a Referral Frenzy."

Practice your outreach and connect with or follow me on LinkedIn at www.linkedin.com/in/fordsaeks.

7. **Join business groups** like Vistage® International and Entrepreneurs' Organization (EO) that also provide training or mastermind components as part of their agenda, however, just like the social examples, you'll have access to individuals who can refer you. I'm an EO member, so if you are too, let's connect.

8. **Host your own networking event or series.** This can be a great way to introduce your business to other local businesses and to build your network.

9. Offer to **sponsor a local event** or organization. This can help you get your business in front of a large audience and can also be a great way to connect with other businesses.

10. Join a local business accelerator or **incubator program**. These programs often provide networking opportunities and access to mentors and other resources.

11. **Collaborate** with other businesses on a project or event. This can help you build relationships and create new opportunities for your business.

12. Offer to **give a presentation or workshop** at a local event or organization. This can help you establish yourself as an expert in your field and can also be a great way to connect with other businesses.

Yada... Yada... now what?

It's not hard. Open Google and search your local community for groups from the previous list. Check out their websites for a calendar of events and attend as a guest.

"But Ford... I'm not a people person."

I can relate. Believe it or not, I'm more of an introvert. Once I discovered a few networking tips and conversation starters in the following lists, networking became more fun, valuable, and a profitable endeavor.

Networking is about building relationships. Be reciprocal, avoid coming on too strong, or hard selling. There are two components to a successful networking experience. The first is to choose the right group or event and the second is to develop the right skills and a plan of action.

Let's discuss a few different ways that you can find the right networking group in your area and then we'll dive into necessary skills

A Dozen Power Networking Tips:

1. Be **prepared** to talk about your business and what makes it unique. Have a brief elevator pitch ready to share with others, highlighting your key services or products and the benefits they offer.

2. Be **open to new opportunities** and connections. Don't be afraid to talk to new people and explore potential partnerships or collaborations.

3. Be **professional and respectful**. Treat others with kindness and respect and be sure to follow up with people you meet after the event to maintain the connection.

4. Ask **open-ended questions**. In case this concept is newer to you, this means avoiding questions that can be answered with a "yes" or "no." For example: "Do you enjoy what you do?" vs "What do you like best about what you do?"

5. Be a **good listener**. Pay attention to what others are saying and ask thoughtful questions to show your interest in their business and experiences.

6. Be **authentic and genuine**. Be yourself and be transparent about your business, its goals, and what you're looking to achieve through networking.

7. Be **willing to give** as well as receive. Networking is a two-way street, so be open to offering help or advice to others and be prepared to accept help or advice in return.

8. **Take Notes.** It's helpful to use your cell phone for video, pictures, or voice memos. Jot down something unique about your conversation so when you follow up, you'll have something to refer to.

9. **Stay organized.** Keep track of the people you meet and the connections you make, so you can follow up and stay in touch with the most valuable contacts. If you have a Client Relationship Management database, add their contact details. Organize your prospect list.

    I like to use an ABC ranking system: A - Hot leads that you should follow up on within a few days. B - Medium leads which are important but not essential to work on immediately. C - You can wait to contact these people because it likely won't lead to anything

10. **Follow up with people you meet.** After the event, be sure to send a quick follow-up email or message to the people you met, thanking them for their time and offering to connect further.

    Example: "It was great meeting you at the chamber event last Tuesday. I hope your dog is feeling better after breaking into the garbage."

    Not only will it show that you were listening and truly engaged in your conversation, it may also trigger their memory so they know who you are when you follow up.

11. **Shoot for quality** over quantity interactions by setting a goal of how many people you'll truly connect with (3-5 is reasonable and takes the pressure off).

12. Be **consistent**. Attend regular networking events and stay engaged with your network to build strong, lasting relationships over time.

Conversation Starters:

- *What brings you to this event today?*

- *What do you enjoy most about your work?*

- *What are some recent projects or accomplishments your business is proud of?*

- *What is the biggest challenge your business is facing right now?*

- *What is your business's biggest strength or differentiator?*

- *Have you attended this event before, or is this your first time?*

- *What do you hope to gain from networking with other business owners?*

- *Are there any upcoming industry events or conferences you're looking forward to?*

There you have it.

We covered:

- Four Ways Why Networking Is Essential

- A Dozen Ways to Find Opportunities to Network

- A Dozen Power Networking Tips

- Eight Conversation Starters

No excuses, please.

And finally, be patient. Building a strong network takes time, so be persistent and keep working at it to see results. The most important thing to remember about networking is that it's not one-sided.

Yes, you are looking to improve your business… but so is everyone else. Don't be selfish and expect everyone to jump at the opportunity to help you if you don't do the same for them. Listen more than you speak, and always ask how you can help someone.

Chapter 25: Creating 5-Star Customer Experiences

All the marketing in the world can't overcome poor customer service...
The best marketing strategy is delivering exceptional customer
experiences.

Avoid these costly mistakes that will damage the customer experience:

- Failing to provide excellent customer service throughout the customer journey. This can include things like being unhelpful, unresponsive, or rude to customers.

- Not offering a wide range of products or services. This can leave customers feeling frustrated or unsatisfied if they are unable to find what they are looking for.

- Not making it easy for customers to find and navigate your business. This can include things like having a poorly designed website or not being listed on popular online directories and map services.

- Not keeping your premises clean and well-maintained. This can create a negative impression and make customers less likely to return.

- Not being responsive to customer feedback and suggestions. This can make customers feel like their opinions and needs are not being taken into account, which can damage the relationship between the business and its customers.

Overall, it is important for businesses to avoid these mistakes in order to maintain a positive relationship with their customers and provide a high-quality customer experience.

How to Create 5-Star Customer Experiences

Improving the customer experience is important for local businesses because it can help to increase customer satisfaction, loyalty, and overall revenue.

136

A positive customer experience can also help to differentiate a business from its competitors and make it more likely that customers will choose to do business with them.

In order to improve the customer experience, it is important for businesses to focus on providing high-quality products or services, as well as offering excellent customer service. This can involve things like offering personalized assistance, being attentive to customer needs, and being willing to go the extra mile to make sure that customers are happy.

Another key element of improving the customer experience is ensuring that your business is easy to find and navigate. This means having a clear and easy-to-use website, as well as making sure that your business is listed on popular online directories and map services. This can help to make it easier for customers to find your business and learn more about what you offer.

Overall, there are many ways that local businesses can improve the customer experience and doing so can have a number of benefits for both the business and its customers.

Here are a few tips on improving the customer experience:

1. Make sure that your business is easy to find and navigate. This means having a clear and concise website, as well as making sure that your business is listed on popular online directories and map services.

2. Provide excellent customer service. This means being friendly, helpful, and attentive to the needs of your customers.

3. Offer a wide range of products or services. This will give customers more options and make it more likely that they will find something that they are looking for.

4. Keep your premises clean and well-maintained. A clean and well-organized business is more inviting and can improve the overall customer experience.

5. Consider offering additional services, such as free Wi-Fi or a loyalty program. These extras can help to make your business stand out and provide added value to your customers.

6. Be responsive to customer feedback and suggestions. This can help you to identify areas where you can improve and can also help to build trust and strengthen your relationship with your customers.

Improving the customer experience is crucial for businesses, as it can increase customer satisfaction, loyalty, and overall revenue. By avoiding costly mistakes that can damage the customer experience and implementing these strategies, franchises can create 5-star customer experiences and differentiate themselves from the competition.

Chapter 26: The Mystery of the Missing Sales: How Secret Shoppers Can Help

We've already explored common mistakes some businesses make that damage the customer experience. In this chapter, we'll explore the benefits of secret shoppers.

Let's take a look at a case study.

A particular local franchise business, which will remain nameless, had seen a steady decline in customer satisfaction and decided to try something new. They hired a mystery shopper to come in and observe their employees' interactions with customers, as well as the overall atmosphere of the store.

As soon as the mystery shopper entered, they noticed how friendly everyone was, from the cashiers to the managers. It seemed that this was a great place for customers to shop and get service. However, things weren't perfect; there were still some areas that needed improvement.

The mystery shopper observed closely how each employee handled different situations with customers: some didn't seem too interested in helping while others always had smiles on their faces when engaging with people.

They also noted discrepancies between what was displayed on menus versus what was actually offered at checkout counters — which could be confusing for customers since it wasn't clear if prices were accurate or not.

In addition, they also looked into operations such as cleanliness of store facilities, order accuracy when preparing items like sandwiches or salads, speed of service, delivery times, etcetera - all which contribute towards providing an excellent experience for patrons visiting this franchise business location.

After spending time observing over several days (and even tasting some items off-menu!), it became evident that changes needed to be made - both big and small - if this franchise wanted to improve its customer experience so more people would return again and again!

Based on all these observations by the mystery shopper, management at this franchise took actionable steps towards improving certain areas of their service model such as introducing better training programs for staff members handling customer interactions (which proved useful!), offering discounts based on loyalty points earned rather than just random offers throughout the year, etcetera.

These efforts combined helped them achieve success in becoming one of the most popular franchises around town! Mystery shopping definitely provided valuable insights into ways they could better serve their audience — making them realize its effectiveness firsthand!

Benefits of Mystery Shopping Your Locations

Mystery shopping can help a business succeed in several ways. First, it provides valuable insights into the customer experience, allowing the business to identify areas for improvement and make changes to enhance the customer experience. This can lead to increased customer satisfaction and loyalty, which can translate into increased sales and revenue.

Second, mystery shopping can help a business identify and address any issues with employees, such as poor customer service or lack of knowledge about the business's products or services. This can help improve the overall quality of the customer experience, leading to increased customer satisfaction and loyalty.

Third, mystery shopping can provide valuable data and insights that can be used to make data-driven business decisions. For example, a business can use mystery shopping data to identify trends and patterns in customer behavior and preferences, which can be used to inform marketing and sales strategies.

Overall, mystery shopping can be a valuable tool for businesses looking to improve their customer experience, identify and address employee issues, and make data-driven business decisions

Here are some ideas you can use. Obviously, you as the owner can't mystery shop in-person because you're not a secret. Yes, I wrote that, but you can get a friend or even hire a professional secret shopper.

1. Visit the business in person and pretend to be a regular customer. Observe the cleanliness of the premises, the friendliness and helpfulness of the staff, and the overall customer experience.

2. Call the business on the phone and inquire about a product or service. Evaluate the phone manners of the person who answers, as well as their ability to provide helpful and accurate information.

3. Place an order online or through the business's mobile app, and evaluate the ease of use of the platform, the speed of delivery, and the accuracy of the order.

4. Visit the business's website and social media pages, and evaluate the design and content of the site, as well as the responsiveness of the business to customer inquiries and complaints.

5. Ask friends and family members who have visited the business to provide their feedback on their experiences. This can provide valuable insights into the business's customer service and overall reputation.

Consider using secret shoppers to improve the customer experience at your franchise. They can provide valuable insights, help you identify and address employee issues, and allow you to make data-driven business decisions.

Hire a professional or ask a friend to visit your business in person and report on the customer experience. It could be just the boost your franchise needs!

ACCELERATE

Chapter 27: You Got Them, Now Keep Them

Improving Customer Loyalty by Improving the Customer Experience (CX)

Diagnose before you prescribe. This means it's important to journey map (diagnose) your customer experience from all touchpoints, and then ensure you have a strategy (prescribe).

Customer Service isn't a department... everyone in your business, and at every touchpoint in the customer journey, has an opportunity to deliver exceptional service.

Tips for creating a customer journey map:

1. **Define your customer segments:** Start by identifying the different types of customers you have and creating personas for each segment. This will help you understand their needs, pain points, and goals. We've discussed this throughout the book.

2. **Identify all touchpoints:** Think about all the different ways your customers interact with your company, including online and offline channels. These are your touchpoints.

3. **Map the journey:** Plot out the steps your prospects and customers take from awareness to loyalty. This includes everything from their initial discovery of your company to post-purchase follow-up.

4. **Look for patterns:** As you map out the journey, look for patterns and opportunities for improvement. Where do customers tend to drop off or get stuck? How can you make their experience more seamless or efficient?

5. **Involve your team:** Get input from your team members who interact with customers on a regular basis. They can provide valuable insights into the customer experience.

6. **Test and iterate:** Once you have a draft of your journey map, test it out with a small group of customers to get their feedback. Use this feedback to fine-tune your map and make any necessary changes.

You can drive traffic to your business all day, every day, but what happens once the potential customers get there?

As a local franchise, it's important to maintain a positive reputation in your community. This can be especially challenging in today's digital age, where it's easy for customers to share their experiences with a wider audience through online review sites and social media.

One negative review can have a significant impact on a business's reputation and ultimately your bottom line. Negative reviews can discourage potential customers from giving you the chance to earn their business and can even drive away loyal customers.

In some cases, just a single negative review can be enough to significantly hurt a business's reputation and cause a decline in revenue. (Please see Chapter 20, "TABOO TOPICS," to help with your online reputation management.)

To avoid the negative consequences of a bad review, it's important to focus on delivering high-quality products or services and provide excellent customer service. You may be thinking, well DUH, Ford…

I know you understand how important this topic is, so how much training do your managers and staff get about the importance of delivering great customer experiences? Is it consistently reinforced? Think back to when we discussed Net Promotor Score (NPS). That rating metric tells the real story of perception vs reality.

A happy customer will tell a few people, but an unsatisfied customer will tell the world.

It's important for businesses to take customer complaints and negative reviews seriously and to respond in a timely and appropriate manner.

I recently featured Customer Experience Expert, **Shep Hyken**, on an episode of *FORDIFY LIVE*, where we discussed how to turn moments of misery (bad CX) into moments of magic (great CX), especially as it relates to overcoming a fumble.

Five step process to help turn a fumble into a positive experience:

1. **Acknowledge:** Every person wants to be heard. When a customer approaches you with a problem, acknowledge the issue rather than trying to explain it away.

2. **Apologize:** Whether the problem is real or not, apologize to the customer. Tell them you're sorry that they are having a less than stellar experience.

3. **Fix it or Discuss a Resolution:** You may not have the power to fix the problem but find someone who does and let the customer know that steps are being taken to resolve their issue.

4. **Be Positive / Have a Good Attitude:** Never argue with the client but rather stay positive so the customer stays calm.

5. **Urgency / Quick Action:** Let the customer know when it will be fixed, and if you can't give a specific time or date, let them know when you (or someone else) will follow up with them.

That's it, just five steps that will keep your customers satisfied and coming back.

Watch the full Episode at Fordify.TV
Create Amazing Customer Experiences by Turning Misery into Magic
bit.ly/cx-moments-of-magic

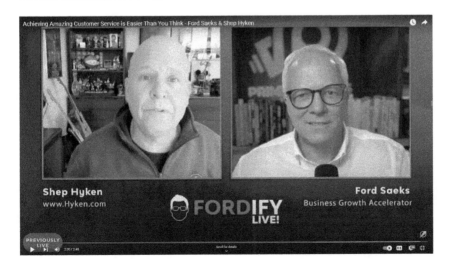

By going above and beyond, even just a tiny bit above average, to meet the needs and expectations of our customers, we can reduce the likelihood of receiving negative reviews and maintain a positive reputation in our local community.

So please, before you continue to invest in more methods of marketing for your business, make sure that you deliver a solid product or service, and that your staff (every single one of them) is trained to deliver top-notch service to your potential and existing customers.

You don't have to be perfect; you just have to be a bit better than your competition. I'm not saying lower the bar, I'm saying that customers just want to feel heard and appreciated... even during a customer service fumble or blunder.

Chapter 28: Mastering Your Marketing Calendar

James owned a small local services franchise in the heart of the city. Despite being in business for several years, he was struggling to keep up with his competitors and attract more customers. He knew that marketing could help him reach more people but wasn't sure where to start or how to manage it all.

One day, James got an idea: create a marketing calendar! With this plan in place, he could easily track when to post on social media channels and send out newsletters or emails about his business. He also planned discounts and promotions around certain dates so that customers would be more likely to purchase from him at those times.

Once the calendar was set up, James started seeing results almost immediately — more traffic coming into his store as well as increased sales! People were excited about the deals they saw online and were happy to take advantage of them while they had the chance.

After a few months of having a successful marketing strategy in place, James's customer base had grown significantly with many new faces visiting his shop each week! It seemed like the combination of an effective digital presence along with timely promotions had done wonders for James's business - proving just how powerful a good marketing calendar can be!

Creating a marketing calendar for a local franchisee is a great way to plan and organize your marketing efforts.

Here are the main steps to help you master your local store marketing calendar:

1. **Determine your marketing goals:** Before creating your marketing calendar, it's important to have a clear understanding of what you want to achieve through your marketing efforts. For example, are you looking to increase local brand awareness, drive foot traffic to your store or to your location's website, or promote a new product or service?

2. **Identify your target audience:** Knowing who you are trying to reach with your marketing efforts will help you create campaigns and messages that resonate with your target audience. Consider factors

such as age, gender, income level, and interests when identifying your target audience.

3. **Select your marketing channels:** Once you have a clear understanding of your goals and target audience, you can choose the marketing channels that will be most effective in reaching them. Some common channels for local franchisees include email marketing, social media, and local print and online advertising.

4. **Plan your campaigns and promotions:** After you have chosen your marketing channels, you can start planning your campaigns and promotions. Consider the key dates and events that are relevant to your business, such as holidays, local events, and special promotions, and plan your campaigns and promotions around these dates.

5. **Create a timeline:** Once you have planned out your campaigns and promotions, you can create a timeline to organize your efforts and ensure that everything is executed smoothly. Include key dates and deadlines, such as the start and end dates for campaigns, the deadline for creating marketing materials, and any other important dates.

6. **Monitor and evaluate your results:** As you execute your marketing calendar, it's important to monitor and evaluate your results to see what is working and what isn't. Use metrics such as website traffic, social media engagement, and sales data to track your progress and make adjustments as needed.

Here is an example of a simple marketing calendar organized by month:

January:

- Review marketing goals and KPIs

- Create content calendar for the month

- Plan and schedule social media posts

- Update website with new products and promotions

February:

- Monitor and respond to online reviews

- Evaluate the effectiveness of January's marketing efforts

- Create email marketing campaign for Valentine's Day

- Plan and schedule social media posts promoting Valentine's Day specials

March:

- Review marketing goals and KPIs

- Create content calendar for the month

- Plan and schedule social media posts

- Update website with new products and promotions

April:

- Monitor and respond to online reviews

- Evaluate the effectiveness of March's marketing efforts

- Create email marketing campaign for Easter

- Plan and schedule social media posts promoting Easter specials

and so on...

As you can see, this marketing calendar includes a mix of regular monthly tasks, such as reviewing goals and KPIs and creating content, as well as special campaigns and promotions for key dates and events. By organizing your marketing efforts in this way, you can ensure that you are consistently working towards your goals and reaching your target audience.

PART IV — BECOME A SELLING SENSATION AND BOOST YOUR SALES

Chapter 29: Connect, Convert, and Close

In this section, we'll cover the key elements of the selling process, including prospecting, presenting, and closing the sale.

But it's not just about those three steps — we'll also dive into the importance of understanding your customers and their needs, building relationships, overcoming objections, providing value, and a whole lot more.

Whether you're a seasoned sales professional or new to the field, we'll be continuing our journey and equip you with the tools and strategies you need to connect, convert, and close more sales, and at higher profitability.

We all know how important sales and marketing are for the success and growth of your businesses. It's kind of like oxygen for a plant — it's essential for survival and growth. Without effective sales and marketing, a business won't be able to reach its target audience and sell its products or services.

In today's competitive market, it takes more than just a great product or service to win over customers. It's about building relationships and earning their trust, and that happens at the local level. Read that sentence again...

That's where the art of connecting comes in. We'll explore how to establish a strong connection with your prospects, creating a foundation for a successful sale.

Next, it's time to convert those connections into paying customers. You'll discover the tools and strategies you need to persuade and influence your prospects, overcome objections, and seal the deal.

Finally, we'll explore how to close the sale and secure the business. With this expert guidance, you'll be able to confidently navigate the selling process and close more deals than ever before... regardless of if your franchise is B2B or B2C.

But before we dive into all of that, it's important to understand the key distinctions between marketing and sales, as well as the main phases in the sales process.

MARKETING is all about promoting a business's products or services to potential customers and increasing brand awareness, while **SALES** is about actually selling those products or services to those customers.

We'll start by covering the differences between marketing and sales, and then move on to the main phases of the sales process — Prospecting, Qualifying, Presenting, and Closing.

Are you ready to master the art of selling and take your business to the next level? Let's get started.

Chapter 30: The Dynamic Duo of Local Franchise Success: Marketing & Sales

I've added this chapter because some of you may be new to marketing and sales, where many others are rock stars!

This entire book has been dedicated to helping you improve your local area marketing and sales efforts, and there's a ton of overlapping content.

So, for clarity purposes, let's all agree that...

Marketing and sales are two sides of the same coin.

Marketing and sales are two related but distinct activities that are essential for the success of any business.

Marketing is the process of creating and promoting a product or service to potential customers. This can include activities such as market research, product development, advertising, and public relations.

The goal of marketing is to create awareness and interest in a product or service and to generate leads that can be passed on to the sales team.

Sales, on the other hand, is the process of converting leads into paying customers. This involves activities such as making contact with potential customers, presenting the product or service, addressing any concerns or objections, and negotiating a sale.

The goal of the sales team is to close deals and generate revenue for the business.

For example....

Imagine you own a franchise of a popular quick service restaurant (QSR) in your town.

Your local **marketing team** is responsible for using your brand's templated and approved promotional materials and campaigns to get people interested in coming to your restaurant.

They (CORPORATE) provide branded ads that highlight your delicious menu items or special deals, LTOs, or create social media templates that showcase your restaurant's atmosphere and vibe. Their goal of marketing is to attract potential customers and create local brand awareness in the local community.

On the other hand, your local **sales team** is focused on converting those potential customers into actual paying customers.

They might greet customers as they come in the door, take their orders, and handle any questions or concerns they might have.

Their goal is to provide excellent customer service and make sure that customers have a positive experience at your restaurant so that they'll come back and recommend your franchise business to others.

Both marketing and sales are essential to the success of your franchise business. Marketing helps to bring in new customers and create a strong brand presence in the community, while sales efforts ensure that those customers have a great experience and are more likely to return in the future.

Chapter 31: The Hunt for New Business & Cultivating Current Relationships

Hunting for New Business and Farming Existing Customers: A Balanced Approach to Local Sales Success

In the context of sales, the terms "hunters" and "farmers" refer to two different approaches to acquiring and servicing customers. This chapter is more targeted towards franchise brands that prospect and sell services, but the concept can also be applied to retail location teams too.

Sales hunters are typically focused on actively seeking out and pursuing new business opportunities.

They tend to be proactive and aggressive in their approach to sales and are often responsible for finding and converting new leads into paying customers.

Sales farmers, on the other hand, are more focused on building and maintaining relationships with existing customers.

They may work to upsell or cross-sell additional products or services to these customers or simply work to ensure that the customer remains satisfied with their current purchase. Farmers may also work to identify potential new business opportunities within their existing customer base.

Imagine a small dessert shop that has been in business for a few years and has a loyal customer base. The owner, Maria, knows that she needs to bring in new business to keep the bakery growing, but she also knows that she can't afford to neglect her existing customers.

To hunt for new business, Maria decides to participate in a local food fair with her food truck, where she can showcase her bakery's products and meet potential new customers. She also reaches out to local businesses to see if they might be interested in placing bulk orders for office events or meetings.

At the same time, Maria is also focused on farming her existing customers. She regularly sends newsletters and updates to her email list, highlighting new products and special deals.

She also makes an effort to engage with her customers on her brand approved social media, responding to comments and questions in a timely manner.

By combining these two approaches, Maria is able to bring in new business while also strengthening her relationships with her existing customers. This helps to ensure that the dessert shop and food truck remain successful and continue to grow.

Both hunters and farmers are important for the success of a team, and the right mix of both approaches will depend on the needs and goals of your business.

Some franchise brands may place a greater emphasis on hunting for new business, while others may prioritize farming existing customers. What about your salespeople, are they hunters or farmers?

Chapter 32: Navigating the Path of Prospecting, Qualifying, Presenting, and Closing

The Road to Successful Sales — the Four Main Phases of the Sales Process *(cont. from chapter 30)*

The hunt is on:

Identifying potential customers — **Prospecting**

The first phase in the sales process is prospecting, which is the process of finding and identifying potential customers. This involves researching and identifying target markets, developing a list of potential leads, and reaching out to them to initiate the sales process.

In a local business, this may involve networking with community organizations, participating in local events, and using online marketing strategies to reach potential customers.

Size them up:

Evaluating the potential of a lead — **Qualifying**

The next phase is qualification, which involves evaluating the potential of a lead to determine whether they are a good fit for your product or service. This involves asking questions, listening to their needs, and determining whether they have the budget and authority to make a purchase. By carefully qualifying leads, you can save time and resources by focusing on the most promising opportunities.

Sell the sizzle:

Showcasing your value proposition — **Presenting**

The third phase is the presentation, which is the process of presenting your product or service to the customer in a way that demonstrates its value and addresses their needs.

This may involve giving a presentation, providing a demo, or making an offer. In a local business, it's important to showcase your unique value proposition and emphasize the personal touch and attention to detail that you offer.

Seal the deal:

Persuading the customer to make a purchase — **Closing**

The final phase in the sales process is closing, which is the process of persuading the customer to make a purchase. This may involve negotiating terms, addressing any objections, and getting the customer to commit to a purchase.

In a local business, it can be helpful to build relationships with customers and offer personalized incentives to close the deal.

By understanding and optimizing each of these phases, you can accelerate your sales and achieve better results in your local business.

In the following chapters, we'll dive deeper into each of these phases and explore strategies for improving them. Stay tuned!

Chapter 33: The Hurdles Salespeople Have to Jump

As the world continues to navigate beyond the "new normal," salespeople are faced with a unique set of challenges.

Gone are the days of predictable markets and easy closes. Instead, salespeople must navigate a landscape of fierce competition, economic uncertainty, and difficult or uninterested customers.

But with the right strategies and mindset (reread PART I of this book), these hurdles can be overcome.

So, let's get started and jump over those hurdles with confidence and grace. There are several challenges that salespeople may face today, including:

1. **Competition:** With many businesses offering similar products or services, salespeople may face intense competition from other companies.

2. **Economic uncertainty:** Economic downturns or other market changes can affect a salesperson's ability to close deals and meet quotas.

3. **Difficult or uninterested customers:** Salespeople may encounter customers who are difficult to persuade or simply not interested in the product or service being offered.

4. **Time management:** Salespeople often have a lot of responsibilities and may struggle to manage their time effectively.

5. **Limited resources:** Salespeople may have limited resources, such as budget or access to information, which can hinder their ability to effectively sell.

6. **Changing market trends:** Staying up to date on market trends and adapting to changes can be a challenge for salespeople.

It's important to remember that sales is an exciting and rewarding profession. Like an acrobat in the circus, salespeople must be agile and adaptable to succeed.

By being aware of the challenges that may come our way and developing strategies to overcome them, we can find success in the changing market landscape.

Let's soar like trapeze artists, vault over those hurdles, and land on the other side with sales success.

Chapter 34: Selling Superpowers: The Essential Skills for Closing Deals & Building Relationships

Sales is more than just selling products and services to customers. It's a challenging and rewarding career that requires a unique set of skills and abilities.

From persuasive communication and efficient time management to adaptability and problem-solving, the skills needed for successful selling are varied and multifaceted.

Whether your franchise location is selling products, services, or both, the ability to connect with customers, persuade them to make a purchase, and provide excellent service are all essential for success. So, what are the key skills that every salesperson should have in their tool kit?

Let's look at the top 10 skills needed for selling success.

1. **Communication skills:** The ability to clearly and effectively communicate with potential customers is essential for building trust and establishing rapport.

2. **Persuasion skills:** Salespeople need to be able to persuade and influence potential customers to make a purchase.

3. **Negotiation skills:** The ability to negotiate terms and pricing with customers is an important part of the sales process.

4. **Time management skills:** Salespeople need to be able to manage their time effectively in order to efficiently meet their sales goals.

5. **Organizational skills:** Salespeople need to be able to keep track of multiple leads and customers and be able to prioritize their tasks accordingly.

6. **Problem-solving skills:** Salespeople often encounter challenges and objections from potential customers and need to be able to come up with creative solutions to overcome these obstacles.

7. **Adaptability:** Salespeople need to be able to adapt to changing market conditions and customer needs in order to be successful.

8. **Product knowledge:** Salespeople need to have a thorough understanding of the products or services they are selling in order to effectively communicate their value to potential customers.

9. **Customer service skills:** Salespeople need to be able to provide excellent customer service in order to build relationships and retain customers.

10. **Networking skills:** Salespeople often rely on networking to find new leads and opportunities and need to be able to build and maintain professional relationships in order to be successful.

Here are several interviewing questions that you can use when evaluating potential candidates for a sales position. It's also a good idea to utilize the power of assessments that will help give you insights that you might not get during the interview process.

- Can you describe your sales process and how you approach a new prospect?

- How do you handle objections or objections from potential customers?

- How do you build and maintain relationships with clients?

- Can you provide an example of a time when you successfully met or exceeded your sales targets?

- How do you stay up to date on industry trends and changes?

- What do you think sets you apart from other sales professionals?

- How do you handle rejection or setbacks in the sales process?

- Can you provide an example of a time when you had to adapt your sales approach to meet the needs of a particular customer or market?

- How do you prioritize your sales leads and activities?

- Can you describe a time when you had to handle a difficult customer or situation in the sales process?

These questions will help you get a sense of a candidate's sales approach and style, their ability to handle objections and challenges, and their overall fit for the role.

It's also a good idea to ask open-ended questions that allow candidates to share specific examples and anecdotes, as these will provide valuable insights into their past experiences and abilities.

ACCELERATE

Chapter 35: Selling Faux Pas: The Top 10 Mistakes Salespeople Make (And How to Avoid Them)

Selling can be tough, but it's even tougher when you're making these common mistakes!

From not knowing your product inside and out to forgetting to ask for the sale, these blunders can make even the most seasoned salesperson cringe. But don't worry, I've got you covered.

Check out our list of the top 10 mistakes salespeople make and how to avoid them so you can sell like a pro (without looking like a fool).

1. **Not understanding the customer's needs:** It's important to take the time to really understand the customer's needs and pain points before trying to sell to them. This will help you tailor your pitch and address their concerns more effectively.

2. **Failing to build relationships:** Building relationships with customers is key to successful sales. Take the time to get to know your customers, establish trust, and build rapport.

3. **Not listening:** It's important to listen carefully to the customer and really understand what they're saying. This will help you tailor your response and address their concerns more effectively.

4. **Not following up:** Follow-up is crucial to the sales process. Make sure to follow up with leads and customers to keep the conversation going and keep your business top of mind.

5. **Being pushy or aggressive:** No one likes to be pressured or hustled. Be respectful and let the customer make their own decision at their own pace.

6. **Not being prepared:** Make sure you're well-prepared for sales meetings and presentations. Know your products or services inside and out and have any relevant materials or information ready to go.

7. **Failing to handle objections:** Objections are a natural part of the sales process. Make sure you have strategies in place to handle objections effectively and address the customer's concerns.

8. **Being too focused on the sale:** Remember that the sales process is about more than just closing the deal. Take the time to build relationships and create a positive experience for the customer.

9. **Not setting clear expectations:** Make sure you set clear expectations with the customer from the beginning. This will help you avoid misunderstandings and ensure that both parties are on the same page.

10. **Not following through:** Make sure you follow through on any commitments you make to the customer. This includes delivering on any promises, meeting deadlines, and providing excellent customer service.

In summary, we've all made mistakes in our careers, and sales is no exception. From not properly researching the product we're selling to not following up with leads, it's easy to fall into common pitfalls.

But the good news is that by being aware of these mistakes and taking steps to avoid them, we can improve our sales skills and close more deals.

Remember, we all make mistakes — it's how we learn and grow from them that matters.

Happy selling!

Chapter 36: The Last Man (or Woman) Standing: How Battlefield Promotions Help Fill Leadership Gaps

In a fast-paced industry where staff turnover is high and qualified candidates for management roles are scarce, battlefield promotions can be a lifesaver for organizations looking to fill leadership positions quickly.

By promoting the most experienced and capable employee, businesses can ensure that there is no disruption in their operations and that their teams are being led by capable leaders.

But how does the process of battlefield promotions work? It typically involves identifying the need for a new manager, evaluating the current staff to determine the most qualified candidate, communicating the promotion to the employee, and providing any necessary training or support.

It's important to carefully consider the qualifications and fit of the promoted employee in order to ensure their success in the new role.

While battlefield promotions can provide a quick solution to filling leadership roles, there are also potential drawbacks to consider. These promotions may be limited to the current pool of employees, which may not always yield the most qualified candidate for the position. Additionally, other employees may feel overlooked for the promotion, and the promoted employee may not have the necessary skills or experience to effectively manage a team.

Overall, battlefield promotions can be a useful strategy in industries or organizations that experience high levels of staff turnover, but it's important to carefully weigh the potential pros and cons before implementing this approach.

Pros of battlefield promotions:

1. **Quick solution to filling a leadership role:** In situations where there is high turnover or a lack of qualified candidates for a management position, battlefield promotions can provide a quick solution to filling the role.

2. **Rewards experience and capability:** Battlefield promotions provide an opportunity for experienced and capable employees to be recognized and promoted, which can help to motivate and retain top talent.

3. **Builds leadership skills:** Being promoted to a management role through a battlefield promotion can provide valuable leadership experience and help employees develop new skills.

Cons of battlefield promotions:

1. **Limited pool of candidates:** Battlefield promotions are typically limited to the current pool of employees, which may not always yield the most qualified candidate for the position.

2. **Limited opportunity for other employees:** Battlefield promotions can create a sense of unfairness among other employees who may feel overlooked for the promotion.

3. **Risk of promoting an unprepared employee:** In some cases, the promoted employee may not have the necessary skills or experience to effectively manage a team, which can lead to challenges and setbacks for the organization.

4. **Potential for negative impact on team morale:** If employees feel that promotions are being unfairly awarded or based on personal connections rather than merit, it can have a negative impact on team morale.

Overall, battlefield promotions can be a useful strategy in situations where there is high turnover and a need for a quick solution to filling a leadership role.

However, it's important to carefully consider the potential pros and cons of this approach and to ensure that the promoted employee is qualified and capable of effectively leading the team.

Chapter 37: From Burnout to Breakthrough: Inspiring Your Salespeople to Perform at Their Best

As an owner, manager, or team leader, it is your responsibility to keep your team motivated and focused on achieving their goals. But let's be real — it's not always easy to keep morale high and avoid burnout.

That's why it's important to constantly find new and creative ways to motivate and support your team. After all, a motivated and engaged team is a productive and successful team.

But it's not just about finding the right incentives or perks. It's about understanding what drives your team and finding ways to tap into that motivation.

It's about fostering a positive and supportive work environment that encourages growth and progress. So, let's dive into some strategies for keeping your team motivated, energized, and focused on success.

1. **Set clear and achievable sales goals:** When salespeople have specific targets to work towards, they are more motivated to put in the extra effort to reach them. Make sure the goals are challenging but achievable so that salespeople feel motivated and not discouraged.

2. **Provide ongoing training and support:** Giving salespeople the tools and knowledge they need to succeed can help boost their confidence and motivate them to sell more. Consider providing ongoing training and support to help salespeople stay up to date on the latest products, services, and sales techniques.

3. **Offer incentives and rewards:** Consider offering incentives or rewards for meeting or exceeding sales targets. These could be financial bonuses, vacation days, or other perks.

4. **Recognize and celebrate success:** Recognizing and celebrating sales successes can help motivate salespeople to continue their efforts. Consider hosting team meetings or events to recognize top performers and share success stories.

5. **Encourage teamwork and collaboration:** Creating a positive and supportive team environment can help motivate salespeople to work together and support each other's success. Encourage teamwork and collaboration, and recognize the efforts of the entire team, not just individual performers.

6. **Foster a culture of continuous learning and growth:** Encourage salespeople to take on new challenges and continue learning and growing in their careers. This can help keep them engaged and motivated to sell more.

The acronym CARES will help you inspire and retain minimum wage employees and reduce high turnover:

C: Competitive Compensation - Ensuring that employees are being paid a competitive wage for their job duties. This means offering a wage that is competitive with other companies in the same industry and region.

A: Acknowledge - Acknowledging the contributions and hard work of employees is a powerful way to inspire and retain them. This can be as simple as thanking them for their efforts, or it can involve more formal recognition programs, such as employee of the month awards.

R: Reward Hard Work - Rewarding employees for their hard work. This may involve offering bonuses or other incentives for meeting or exceeding performance goals or offering rewards for exceptional performance.

E: Encourage Open Communication - Creating an open and transparent work environment where employees feel comfortable sharing their ideas and concerns. This means encouraging your team to speak up and actively listening to their feedback and concerns.

S: Support and Encouragement - Providing support and encouragement to help them feel valued and motivated to continue working for you. This may involve providing training and development opportunities, offering flexible work arrangements, and offering support and resources to help employees succeed in their roles.

Overall, these (CARES) strategies will help create a positive work culture that inspires and retains your employees, leading to lower turnover and improved business success.

As a leader, it's your responsibility to keep your team motivated and focused on success. And let's face it, it's not always easy to do that! That's why it's so important to constantly find new and creative ways to motivate and support your team.

A motivated and engaged team is a productive and successful team, right? The strategies in this chapter will help your team feel motivated, engaged, and supported, leading to increased productivity and success.

Remember, it's not just about finding the right perks – it's about understanding what drives your team and finding ways to tap into that motivation. So, get creative and keep your team motivated for success!

Chapter 38: How to Motivate a Team to Provide Better Customer Service

Imagine a world where every customer interaction is a positive one. Where customers leave feeling satisfied, valued, and eager to return. This is the world we can create when we have a team of motivated, customer-focused employees.

Providing excellent customer service requires more than just technical skills and knowledge – it requires a genuine desire to help and serve others.

In this chapter, we will explore how to inspire and motivate our staff to deliver top-notch customer service that leaves a lasting impression on every customer they encounter.

But first. It's important that you hire right. Ultimately it's difficult to teach "give a $#!+" Motivating a staff member who doesn't seem to care about their job can be challenging, but it's not impossible.

There are several ways you can motivate your team to provide better customer service:

1. **Identify the root cause of their lack of motivation:** It's important to understand why the staff member is not motivated before you can address the issue. Are they feeling overwhelmed or burnt out? Do they feel undervalued or unappreciated? By identifying the underlying cause of their lack of motivation, you can tailor your approach to address their specific needs.

2. **Set clear expectations:** Make sure that your team understands the customer service standards that you expect them to uphold. Communicate these expectations clearly and consistently and provide training and resources to help them meet these standards.

3. **Recognize and reward good performance:** When team members provide excellent customer service, make sure to recognize and reward their efforts. This could be through verbal praise, written feedback, or other incentives such as bonuses or promotions.

4. **Offer opportunities for growth and development:** Show your team that you are invested in their professional development by offering training and learning opportunities. This can help them improve their customer service skills and feel more motivated to excel in their roles.

5. **Foster a positive work culture:** A positive work culture can go a long way in motivating your team to provide excellent customer service. This includes creating a respectful, supportive, and inclusive environment where team members feel valued and appreciated.

6. **Encourage open communication:** Encourage your team to share ideas and feedback on how to improve the customer experience. This can help identify areas where your team is struggling and provide an opportunity to address any challenges they may be facing.

7. **Make customer service a priority:** Make it clear that customer service is a top priority for your organization and encourage your team to prioritize it as well. This can help create a customer-centric culture and motivate your team to go above and beyond for your customers.

Give them additional training because it will help you staff members learn the skills and knowledge they need to perform provide outstanding service. Training can also foster a positive work culture by showing staff that the organization values their development and is committed to helping them succeed.

Bonus Exercises you can use with your staff to help improve their customer service training:

Role-playing: Have staff members take turns role-playing different customer service scenarios, such as handling a complaint or assisting a customer with a question. This can help them practice and improve their communication and problem-solving skills.

Mystery shopper: Have a staff member act as a "mystery shopper" and assess the customer service they receive from other team members. This can help them understand the customer's perspective and identify areas for improvement. We'll explored Mystery Shopping in chapter 26.

Customer service scavenger hunt: Create a list of customer service tasks or challenges for staff members to complete, such as greeting every customer who enters the store or finding a solution to a customer's problem. This can be a fun way to encourage staff to think creatively and practice their customer service skills

In Summary, Motivating and inspiring your staff to provide excellent customer service is all about attitude and effort. By building a culture of motivation, communication, and excellence, you will create a workplace where everyone is motivated to give their best, and where your customers always feel valued and appreciated.

We'll explore ways to improve engagement and retention in the next chapter.

Chapter 39: 12 Ways to Inspire and Retain Minimum Wage Employees and Reduce Turnover

Did the title of this chapter get your attention? The good news is that these strategies work to help you retain ALL levels of staff, not just those at lower wage positions.

Okay. We can all agree that finding, engaging, and retaining top talent can be a struggle, especially for local businesses where much of their staff may be starting at lower wages.

I understand the unique challenges you face and want to provide you with practical strategies to help you build and maintain a strong and effective team, for all your departments, not just marketing and sales. That's why we've written this chapter specifically for you.

I have other books, training programs, and keynote presentations specifically on **"Winning Workforce Strategies"** you or your corporate brand may want to take advantage of, but I'd be doing you a disservice if I didn't at least put a couple chapters in *ACCELERATE* to help you with staffing challenges. I hope you find them valuable.

Here's a dozen strategies that can help you inspire and retain your staff:

1. **Set goals:** Help employees set specific, achievable goals for themselves, both short-term and long-term. This can give them something to work towards and provide motivation.

2. **Offer competitive compensation:** Make sure that your employees are being fairly compensated for their work. This can help to attract and retain top talent and reduce turnover.

3. **Foster a positive work culture:** Create a positive and supportive work environment that values diversity, inclusivity, and open communication. This can help employees feel more connected to their work and colleagues, which can increase motivation and engagement.

4. **Provide opportunities for growth and development:** Offer employees opportunities for training, skill development, and advancement. This can help employees feel more invested in their work and give them a sense of purpose and meaning.

5. **Offer flexible schedules:** Allow employees flexibility in their work schedules and encourage them to take breaks when needed. This can help reduce stress and improve overall well-being.

6. **Recognize and reward hard work:** Acknowledge and reward the hard work and dedication of your employees. This can include things like promotions, raises, and public recognition.

7. **Provide support and resources:** Offer resources such as job training, mentorship, and access to necessary tools and equipment to help employees perform their jobs effectively.

8. **Encourage open communication:** Encourage open and honest communication between employees and management. This can help employees feel valued and heard, which can increase job satisfaction and retention.

9. **Foster teamwork and collaboration:** Encourage teamwork and collaboration among employees and create a sense of community in the workplace. This can help employees feel more connected to their colleagues and the organization, which can increase motivation and engagement.

10. **Implement flexible scheduling:** Consider offering flexible scheduling options, such as part-time or shift work, to help employees balance their work and personal commitments. This can increase job satisfaction and reduce turnover.

11. **Offer benefits and perks:** Offer benefits and perks such as healthcare, retirement plans, and employee discounts to help attract and retain employees.

12. **Promote work-life integration:** Encourage employees to find a balance between their work and personal lives. This can help reduce stress and improve overall well-being, which can increase job satisfaction and retention.

It's important to remember that your employees are the foundation of your business. By investing in their growth and well-being, you are not only helping them achieve their full potential, but you are also setting your business up for long-term success.

By implementing strategies that we've discussed in this chapter, you can inspire and motivate ALL your employees to be their best selves.

This will ultimately lead to increased retention, productivity, and overall success for your franchise units. So, don't forget to take the time to invest in and support your team — they are the key to your success!

Chapter 40: The Power of Sales Training: Unlocking Your Potential and Achieving Success

Sales training is an opportunity to unleash the full potential of your team and help them become masters of persuasion!

By gaining the knowledge, skills, and strategies necessary for success, you can learn how to effectively communicate and connect with potential customers, understand their needs and motivations, and overcome any objections that may arise.

You'll also have the chance to develop a deep understanding of your products or services and learn how to present them in the most compelling way possible.

Plus, you'll discover how to manage and grow a successful sales pipeline and make the most of the latest sales technologies and tools.

Sales Training Fundamentals

1. **Start with the basics:** Make sure that all team members have a solid understanding of your products or services, as well as your company's sales process and techniques.

2. **Provide ongoing training and support:** Sales skills and techniques can evolve over time, so it's important to provide regular training and support to help your team stay up to date and develop their skills.

3. **Encourage practice and feedback:** Provide opportunities for team members to practice their sales skills and techniques and encourage them to seek feedback from managers and peers to identify areas for improvement.

4. **Help team members develop their own sales style:** Encourage team members to find their own unique selling style and approach and provide support and guidance as needed.

5. **Set clear goals and expectations:** Make sure that your team members understand your sales goals and expectations and provide support and guidance to help them achieve those goals.

6. **Provide resources and tools:** Make sure that your team has access to the resources and tools they need to succeed, such as training materials, customer relationship management (CRM) software, and marketing materials.

7. **Recognize and reward success:** Provide recognition and rewards for team members who excel at sales, which can help to motivate and inspire the rest of the team.

Overall, the key to providing effective sales training is to focus on ongoing support, practice, and development and to provide the tools and resources that your team needs to succeed.

Next, it's time to put theory into practice with these proven sales skills building exercises.

Selling role-playing: Salespeople can practice their sales skills by role-playing different scenarios, such as making a cold call, handling objections, or closing a deal.

Customer service role-play: Salespeople can practice their customer service skills by role-playing different customer scenarios, such as handling complaints, resolving issues, and upselling.

Product knowledge quiz: You could create a quiz to test salespeople's knowledge of your products or services. This could include questions about features, benefits, pricing, and any other relevant details.

Icebreakers: Icebreakers can help salespeople get to know each other and build relationships. You could use activities such as "Two Truths and a Lie" or "Human Knot" to help salespeople bond and have fun.

Sales pitch practice: Salespeople can practice their sales pitches by giving a presentation on a product or service to the group. Other members of the group can provide feedback and suggestions for improvement.

Negotiation simulation: You could create a negotiation simulation where salespeople practice negotiating with a customer or supplier. This could include role-playing different negotiation scenarios and discussing strategies for getting the best deal.

Sales simulation game: You could create a sales simulation game where salespeople compete against each other to see who can make the most sales. This can be a fun way to practice sales skills and see how they stack up against their colleagues.

Team building exercises: Team building exercises can help salespeople work together more effectively and build stronger relationships. You could use activities such as trust falls or problem-solving challenges to help salespeople bond and build trust.

Additional resources to help you and your team improve performance:

- Get a copy of this book for all of your marketing and salespeople. It's a great reference that they should review on a regular basis to improve their marketing and sales performance.

- Check out the resources in the back of the book for additional customized training solutions. Check out: ProfitRichResults.com/product/sales-assessment/

If you're interested in Top Rated Keynote presentations or sales training solutions watch my speaker demo video at www.FranchiseTrainingSolutions.com. Keep in mind, all presentations and interactive workshops are customized for your outcomes, brand, and revenue model.

Here's one of my popular titles for selling success.

Superpower Sales Success: Unleashing Your Inner Sales Champion with Ford Saeks

Learning objectives:

- Understand the key principles of effective sales
- Develop a personalized sales approach
- Identify and overcome common objections
- Practice and refine your sales pitch for authentic connections
- Develop strategies for building long-term customer relationships

Workshop outline:

Day 1:

- Introduction to the principles of effective sales

- Identifying your target audience and tailoring your sales approach

- Developing a personalized sales pitch

- Overcoming common objections

Day 2:

- Building long-term customer relationships

- Practice and feedback sessions

- Developing a personal action plan for continued sales success

Materials provided:

- Custom training guide, handouts, and worksheets

- Access to online resources, support materials, and bonus "how-to" videos

- Presenter: Ford Saeks, CSP, CPAE Hall of Fame Keynote Speaker, experienced sales professional with a proven track record of success

In conclusion, consistent training is essential for salespeople to improve their skills and become more successful in their roles.

It's important to remember that training is not a one-time event, but rather an ongoing process. By regularly practicing techniques such as role-playing, quizzing, icebreakers, pitch practice, negotiation simulations, and team building exercises, salespeople can continuously improve and become more confident in their abilities.

Don't let training fall by the wayside — make it a priority in your organization (ZEEs & ZORs) to ensure the success of your sales team.

Chapter 41: Discovering New Opportunities: The Sales PROSPECTING Phase

Let's keep this simple. The sales process typically consists of FOUR MAIN PHASES:

1. **Prospecting:** identifying and finding potential customers

2. **Qualifying:** evaluating the potential customer's needs and determining if they are a good fit for the product or service being offered

3. **Presenting:** presenting the product or service to the potential customer and addressing their needs and concerns

4. **Closing:** negotiating and finalizing the sale

Each phase involves a different set of activities and goals, but they all contribute to the ultimate goal of making a successful sale.

By understanding and effectively navigating each phase, sales professionals can improve their chances of closing deals and building long-term relationships with customers

Phase 1 of the sales process is all about prospecting, the act of identifying and qualifying potential customers for your business.

As a local business, there are a variety of tactics you can consider to effectively prospect for new customers. From networking events and referrals to cold calling and social media outreach, the options for finding qualified leads are vast. The key is to choose the tactics that align with your business goals and target audience.

So, let's dive into the world of **prospecting** and explore some of the strategies you can use to bring in new business.

1. **Networking:** Attend local events, such as networking events, chamber of commerce meetings, or industry conferences, to meet potential customers and build relationships.

2. **Referrals:** Ask current customers for referrals to other potential customers. You could also offer incentives, such as discounts or

referral fees, to encourage customers to refer others to your business.

3. **Cold calling:** Make phone calls to potential customers to introduce your business and its services. You could also send email or direct mail campaigns to reach out to potential customers.

4. **Online marketing:** Use online marketing techniques, such as search engine optimization, social media marketing, and email marketing, to reach potential customers online.

5. **Partnerships and collaborations:** Partner with other local businesses or organizations to cross-promote your services and reach new customers.

6. **Public speaking presentations:** Offer to speak at local events or workshops to share your expertise and build your reputation as a thought leader in your industry.

7. **Community involvement:** Get involved in your local community by volunteering, attending local events, or sponsoring community organizations. This can help you build relationships and raise awareness of your business.

8. **Direct mail campaigns:** Send targeted direct mail campaigns to potential customers to introduce your business and its services. You could include coupons or special offers to encourage them to try your services.

As you begin prospecting for new customers, consider your brand's guidelines and ensure they align with your business goals and target audience.

Maintain a clear and unwavering focus, cultivate a positive outlook, and persevere with determination as you search for new opportunities to grow your business. Building relationships is key, so be genuine and authentic in your interactions. With the right mindset and tactics (see PART I), you can successfully build a sustainable sales pipeline for your local franchise business.

Chapter 42: Lead Magnet Magic: How to Attract and Convert Local Customers with Valuable Resources

Lead magnets are powerful tools that can help franchisees in any industry, with their local marketing and sales efforts, attract and convert potential customers.

We discussed lead magnets a bit in earlier chapters because lead magnets can be used with inbound and outbound marketing campaigns to generate leads and with salespeople, for cold and warm outreach.

Marketers like me, use all kinds of fancy terms to explain lead magnets, but the purpose is the same with a few nuances, such as:

- **Ethical bribes:** The "ethical" part of this term refers to the fact that the resource or incentive should be truly valuable and relevant to the potential customer, rather than being used as a deceptive or manipulative tactic.

- **Freebies:** These are resources or incentives that are offered for free in exchange for contact information. Examples might include e-books, templates, or sample products.

- **Opt-in incentives:** These are resources or incentives that are offered in exchange for a potential customer opting in to receive emails or other marketing communications.

- **Gated content:** This refers to content that is only accessible after a potential customer provides their contact information. Examples might include webinars, courses, or white papers.

- **Lead generation offers:** These are resources or incentives that are specifically designed to generate leads for a business. Examples might include demos, consultations, or product samples.

- **Bait:** This term is often used to refer to resources or incentives that are used to entice potential customers to provide their contact information. These can include anything from e-books and templates to product samples and webinars.

See. Lots and lots of overlap.

Here's the point. By offering valuable resources or incentives in exchange for contact information, you can build your prospect email lists and generate leads for your sales team to follow up on.

Lead magnets can be especially effective for local marketing and sales, as they allow you to target specific geographic areas and tailor your marketing efforts to the needs and interests of your ideal local customer avatar. Another fancy way of saying customers.

Before you email asking which type is best, I'll answer by saying it really depends on your brand's products and services and focus of the content of the lead magnet, but for sure needs to provide value and answer the top questions in the mind of your prospect.

How to Use Lead Magnets

Here are several ideas and examples, but again, like all marketing tactics, please get approvals from corporate and follow your brand's style guide.

Demos: Offering a demo of your product or service can be a great way to showcase its features and benefits to potential customers. For example, a local software company could offer a demo of their product in exchange for an email address.

Consultations: Offering a personalized consultation or assessment can be a valuable lead magnet for salespeople. This could involve offering a free consultation to assess a potential customer's needs and provide recommendations for products or services that could meet those needs.

White Papers: Providing detailed, research-based reports on a specific topic can be a powerful lead magnet. For example, a local B2B company could offer a white paper on *"Best Ways to Protect Your Business"* in exchange for an email address or through cold outreach.

Research Reports: Sharing research or data on a specific topic can be a compelling lead magnet. For example, you could share a research report on *"Consumer Trends in the Food and Beverage Industry"* in exchange for contact information.

Product Samples: If you're a QSR, fast-casual, or full-service dining brand, then you're well aware of product sampling for prospecting. Offering a sample of your product can be a great way to introduce potential customers to what you have to offer. That's how I fell in love with Duck Donuts! They gave me a sample box of their delicious donuts, and I was hooked. Ten from me on the NPS score.

Checklists: These can be helpful resources that provide a step-by-step guide to completing a task or achieving a specific goal. For example, a local home improvement store could offer a checklist for "A" in exchange for an email address. I have an E.O. member (Entrepreneurs' Organization) in my mastermind forum who is a successful franchisee offering residential and commercial painting services. I emailed him a few titles because he was looking for new titles and topics... Here's what I sent him.

> "Paint Your Way to Perfection: A Guide to Choosing the Right Colors for Your Home"

> "The Essential Checklist for Preparing Your Home for a Fresh Coat of Paint"

> "Before and After Inspiration: See the Transformative Power of a New Coat of Paint"

> "The Ultimate Color Palette: A Collection of the Hottest Painting Trends for 202X"

Templates: Offering customizable templates can be a valuable lead magnet for local businesses. For example, a local marketing agency could offer a template for creating an effective social media strategy in exchange for contact information.

E-books: Providing a comprehensive guide or resource on a specific topic can be a powerful lead magnet. For example, a local restaurant could offer an e-book on *"Healthy Eating for Busy Professionals"* in exchange for an email address.

Webinars: Offering a live or recorded webinar on a relevant topic can be a great way to attract leads and showcase expertise. For example, a local fitness studio could offer a webinar on *"At-Home Workout Strategies"* in exchange for contact information.

Quizzes: Creating a quiz or survey that provides personalized recommendations or results can be a fun and engaging way to capture leads. For example, a local beauty salon could offer a quiz that helps customers discover their "perfect makeup look" in exchange for an email address.

Sample Pack: Offering a sample of a product or service can be a great way to introduce potential customers to what you have to offer. For example, a local coffee shop could offer a sample pack of their most popular blends in exchange for an email address.

Case Studies: Sharing detailed accounts of how your business has successfully helped other customers can be a powerful lead magnet. For example, a local marketing agency could offer case studies of their most successful campaigns in exchange for contact information.

Worksheets: Providing helpful worksheets or printables can be a valuable lead magnet for local businesses. For example, a local financial advisor could offer a worksheet for creating a budget in exchange for an email address.

Courses: Offering a mini-course or tutorial on a relevant topic can be a great way to attract leads and showcase expertise. For example, a local art studio could offer a course on *"Beginning Watercolor Techniques"* in exchange for contact information.

Video Series: Creating a series of short videos on a specific topic can be a compelling lead magnet. For example, a local yoga studio could offer a video series on *"Yoga for Beginners"* in exchange for an email address.

Overall, the key to using lead magnets effectively is to offer something of value that will attract the attention of potential customers and incentivize them to provide their contact information. By doing so, businesses and sales teams can build their lists and generate valuable leads that can be nurtured and converted into sales.

Chapter 43: How to Create Compelling Lead Magnets

Are you ready to take your lead generation efforts to the next level? Just in case you skipped the previous chapter, a lead magnet can be the key to attracting and converting potential customers. But where do you start? Don't worry, we've got you covered.

Follow these simple steps to craft a lead magnet that will have your audience begging for more:

1. **Identify your target audience:** Before you start creating your lead magnet, it's important to know who you are trying to reach. This will help you tailor your content to the needs and interests of your audience.

2. **Determine the purpose of your lead magnet:** Consider what you want to achieve with your lead magnet. Do you want to educate your audience about a specific topic, solve a problem they are facing, or provide them with a valuable resource?

3. **Choose a format:** There are many different formats, as we discussed in the last chapter, you can use for your lead magnet, such as e-books, white papers, webinars, templates, or checklists. Choose the format that best fits your audience and the purpose of your lead magnet. Lead magnets can be used in all phases of the sales process to nurture relationships, help generate referrals, and more.

4. **Create a compelling headline:** Your headline should grab the attention of your audience and clearly communicate the value of your lead magnet. There are all kinds of AI tools that can now help you with headlines. One helpful service at the time of publishing this book is called Jasper. Check it out at www.Jasper.com. Just like any service, do your due diligence before using it.

5. **Outline the content:** Create an outline of the content you will include in your lead magnet. This will help you stay organized and ensure that you cover all the important points.

6. **Write the content:** Use the outline to guide you as you write the content for your lead magnet. Make sure to provide value to your audience and address their needs and interests.

7. **Edit and proofread:** Before you publish your lead magnet, make sure to thoroughly edited and proofread it to ensure that it is error-free and easy to understand.

8. **Promote your lead magnet:** Once your lead magnet is complete, promote it to your target audience through your local page on your franchisee location website, approved local social media, email marketing, or other local marketing channels.

In summary:

Attention all franchise business owners! Are you tired of struggling to generate leads for your company? Well, fear not my friends because lead magnets are here to save the day! By offering valuable and relevant content, you can attract and convert your ideal customers. So go ahead and get creative with your lead magnets — whether it's a witty e-book or a hilarious webinar — the sky's the limit.

Just remember, the key to success is to make your lead magnets so irresistible, even your competition will want to sign up. Happy lead generating.

Did that inspire you to create and use lead magnets? I hope so!

Get My Lead Magnet:

Employment Strategies that Drive Business Growth

Instant access at: ProfitRichResults.com/employment-strategies-report/

Chapter 44: Using Gifts to Build Relationships and Help Create Loyal Fans

Here's another suggestion to help you stand out from the competition and really connect with your potential customers.

Try incorporating gifts into your sales process. Not only are gifts a thoughtful and personalized touch, but they can also serve as a physical reminder of your company and the value you offer.

In this chapter, we'll go over how using gifts during the sales process can actually help boost your local sales efforts. From building trust and rapport with prospects to showing your appreciation for their business, gifts can be an effective tool in your sales tool kit.

So, stick around and let's learn more about how gifts can help with your local sales efforts. It's important to approach the use of gifts in a professional and ethical manner.

Here are a few do's and don'ts to keep in mind when using gifts during the sales process:

Do:

- Personalize the gift to the recipient. This shows that you've taken the time to get to know them and their interests.

- Choose a gift that aligns with your company's values and image. For example, if you're an eco-conscious company, consider a sustainable gift like a reusable water bottle.

- Use the gift as an opportunity to showcase your company's product or service. For example, if you're a bakery, you could give a gift basket filled with your signature pastries.

Don't:

- Use gifts as a bribe or attempt to sway someone's decision with extravagance. This is unethical and can actually backfire.

- Choose a gift that is too expensive or inappropriate for the recipient. It's important to consider your relationship with the person and their preferences.

- Wait until the end of the sales process to give the gift. It's best to present the gift at an appropriate time, such as after a successful meeting or as a follow-up to a positive conversation.

This list of ideas will get you started. There are hundreds of resources online, and I'm sure many in your local community, that can either make them for you or handle the whole process.

1. **Customized gift boxes:** Put together a gift box filled with a selection of branded items, such as T-shirts, hats, and mugs, as well as some non-branded items like snacks or local artisanal products.

2. **Experience packages:** Instead of just giving out physical items, offer an experience package that includes tickets to a local event or a gift certificate for a local restaurant or attraction.

3. **Personalized gifts:** Show your appreciation for your customers by giving them a personalized gift, such as a custom-made piece of jewelry or a personalized piece of artwork.

4. **Unique product bundles:** Create a bundle of your products or services that includes some unique or exclusive items that customers won't be able to get elsewhere.

5. **Fun and unexpected items:** Surprise your customers with something unexpected and fun, like a bundle of novelty items or a box of confetti.

If you're going to use this strategy, I highly recommend the book, *GIFTOLOGY: The Art and Science of Using Gifts to Cut Through the Noise, Increase Referrals, and Strengthen Client Retention* by John Ruhlin. You can get it on Amazon or from your favorite bookseller.

By getting creative with your swag packages, you can create a memorable and appreciated surprise for your customers that will help to build your brand awareness and drive sales.

Chapter 45: From Suspect to Prospect: Navigating the QUALIFICATION Phase

Qualifying is phase 2 in the sales process.

Are you tired of wasting time and resources chasing leads that aren't a good fit for your product or service? The qualification phase is here to save the day!

This crucial step involves carefully evaluating the potential of each lead to determine whether they have the budget, authority, and need for what you're selling.

By asking the right questions and listening to their needs, you can zero in on the most promising opportunities and save yourself a lot of time and energy in the process.

Here's are a few helpful tips to help you improve the performance of your sales efforts during the qualification phase.

1. Ask **questions** to understand the potential customer's needs and challenges. This can help you determine whether your product or service is a good fit for their needs.

2. Determine the potential customer's **budget** and **decision-making authority**. It's important to know whether they have the financial resources and authority to make a purchase.

3. Listen to the potential customer's **needs and concerns**. Pay attention to their pain points and objections and address them in your sales pitch.

4. Evaluate the potential customer's **level of interest** and commitment. Are they actively seeking solutions and ready to move forward with a purchase, or are they still in the research phase?

5. Use a lead qualification form or **checklist** to ensure that you cover all the necessary information. This can help you stay organized and focused during the qualification process.

Don't let your time and resources go to waste chasing leads that just aren't a good fit for your product or service. The qualification phase is here to help you make the most of your efforts!

This important step involves carefully evaluating the potential of each lead to determine if they have the budget, authority, and need for what you're selling.

By asking the right questions and really listening to their (the prospect's) needs, you can focus on the most promising opportunities and save yourself a lot of time and energy in the process. So, don't skip this crucial part of the sales process — it's an essential step that can help you close more deals and grow your business.

Invest a little time and effort in the qualification phase and you'll be amazed at the results!

Chapter 46: Maximizing Your Impact During the Presenting Phase of the Sales Process

The **presentation phase** of the sales process is your time to shine! This is when you get to present your products or services to potential customers in a way that demonstrates their value and addresses their needs.

You might give a presentation, provide a demo, or make an offer — whatever it takes to convince them that you're the best choice.

Show your potential customers that you care about their needs and are willing to go the extra mile to meet them. With a strong presentation, you can turn leads into loyal customers and grow your business.

Tips for effectively presenting your products or services during the third phase (PRESENTING) of the selling process:

1. **Clearly articulate your unique value proposition:** Your unique value proposition is what sets your business apart from competitors and explains why customers should choose you over them.

    For example, if you own a local franchise of a fast-food (QSR) chain, your unique value proposition might be that you offer high-quality, locally sourced ingredients, or that you have a commitment to sustainability and environmental responsibility. Clearly communicating your unique value proposition can help to differentiate your business and convince prospects to choose you.

2. **Highlight the features and benefits of your products or services:** When presenting your products or services, it's important to focus on how they will solve the customer's problems or meet their needs.

    For example, if you own a local franchise of a home cleaning service, you might highlight the convenience and peace of mind that customers can experience by hiring professionals to handle their cleaning tasks.

3. **Use visual aids and demos to make your presentation more engaging and effective:** Visual aids such as slides, charts, and

videos can help to make your presentation more engaging and easier to understand.

For example, you might also consider demonstrating your products or services in action, either in person or through a video. This can help to give prospects a better understanding of how your offerings work and the value they can provide.

4. **Practice your presentation in advance to ensure that you're confident and well-prepared:** This can involve rehearsing your delivery, timing, and any visual aids or demos you will be using.

For example, if you own a local franchise of a gym, you might practice your presentation several times in front of a mirror or with a colleague, paying attention to your body language, pacing, and the use of any visual aids such as slides or videos. Practicing can help to reduce nervousness and ensure that you are able to deliver your presentation smoothly and effectively.

5. **Anticipate and address any objections or concerns that the customer might have:** Customers may have objections or concerns about your products or services, and it's important to anticipate and address these during your presentation.

You might also consider offering incentives or guarantees to address these concerns and provide added value to the customer. *(Don't worry… We've got future chapters that go even deeper on the common objections and overturns too.)*

For example, if you own a local franchise of a home security company, prospects might be concerned about the cost of installation and monthly fees. Anticipating these concerns and addressing them up front can help to build trust and overcome objections.

6. **Make an offer or proposal that addresses the customer's needs and budget:** At the end of your presentation, it's important to make an offer or proposal that addresses the customer's needs and budget.

For example, if you own a local franchise of a home improvement company, you might offer a discount for customers who sign up for a multi-year contract or package deal. By tailoring your offer to the customer's needs and budget, you can increase the chances of securing the business.

Remember, the presentation phase of the sales process is your time to shine! This is when you get to show potential customers the value of your products or services and convince them to make a purchase.

By following some simple tips, such as highlighting the benefits of your offerings and anticipating any objections, you can give a strong and effective presentation that will help you turn leads into loyal customers and grow your business.

A combination of preparation, practice, and enthusiasm will allow you to showcase your offerings in a way that truly resonates with potential clients and customers.

"That sound's great, Ford, but what do I do or say when the prospects give me objections?" Great question, stand up and stretch, grab some water or coffee, and let's explore proven strategies you can adapt to help you overcome any objections and close more sales.

Chapter 47: Authentic Influence: Proven Strategies for Overcoming Sales Objections

Remember, selling is just giving people enough of the right information that they can make an informed decision. It's not about manipulation or tricking them with some fancy or manipulative tactic.

Objections are a natural part of the sales process, but that doesn't mean they have to hold you back. In fact, with the right mindset and preparation, objections can be a chance to shine and build trust with potential customers.

So, how do you handle objections like a pro?

First and foremost, it's important to be proactive. Anticipate potential objections and have authentic responses ready to go. This way, when objections do come up, you'll be able to address them confidently and convincingly.

And remember, objections aren't personal attacks — they're just a chance for your potential customer to get clarification or express their concerns. So, stay calm, listen actively, and use objections as an opportunity to showcase your expertise and build rapport.

With the right approach, you can turn objections into a stepping stone to sales success.

Common FEARS before making a buying decision include:

1. **Fear of risk:** Many people are hesitant to make a purchase if they perceive it as a risk. They may worry about losing money, being disappointed with the product, or experiencing negative consequences.

For example, a prospect may say, "I'm not sure if I want to buy this new product from you (you or your business) because I've never tried it before, and I'm worried it won't work for me."

2. **Fear of failure:** Some people may be hesitant to make a purchase because they fear that the product or service won't live up to their expectations or won't help them achieve their goals.

For example, a prospect may say, "I'm not sure if I want to start my own business because I'm worried that I won't be able to make it successful and it will be a waste of time and effort."

3. **Fear of conflict:** Some people may be hesitant to make a purchase because they fear that it will cause conflict with others, such as their spouse, family, or coworkers.

For example, a prospect may say, "I'm not sure if I want to purchase this membership to your gym because my spouse thinks it's too expensive and I'm afraid it will cause conflict in our relationship."

4. **Fear of the unknown:** Some people may be hesitant to make a purchase because they are uncertain about what to expect or how the product or service will fit into their lives.

For example, a prospect may say, "I'm not sure if I want to try your new restaurant because I've never had this type of food before and I'm not sure if I'll like it."

5. **Fear of being taken advantage of:** Some people may be hesitant to make a purchase because they fear that they will be taken advantage of or scammed.

For example, a prospect may say, "I'm not sure if I want to hire your cleaning service because I'm worried that your team will take advantage of my trust and not do a thorough job."

By understanding these common fears in advance, you and your salespeople can be better prepared to address them and reassure potential customers.

I wish that those five fears were all of the objections, but wait, there's more…

On the following page is a list of the most common sales objections and list of strategies to help you effectively overturn (respond).

It's essential that you modify and adapt your responses to be specific for your products and services. Now's another great time to remind you to utilize the training resources, if any, that are provided to you from your corporate headquarters (ZOR).

Common objections include:

Price: Customers may feel that the product or service is too expensive.

For example, "I understand that your product has a lot of features, but it's too expensive for our budget. Can you offer any discounts or financing options?"

Lack of need: Customers may feel that they do not have a need for the product or service.

For example, "I don't think our business has a need for your product. We already have a similar solution in place that seems to be working fine."

Lack of time: Customers may feel that they do not have the time to invest in the product or service.

For example, "I'm sorry, but we don't have the time or resources to invest in implementing your product right now. We have a lot of other projects that need to be completed first."

Competitor offerings: Customers may be considering a competing product or service.

For example, "I've looked at your product and it seems great, but a competitor has offered us a similar solution at a lower price point. I'm not sure if we can justify the extra cost for your product."

Risk: Customers may be concerned about the risk of purchasing the product or service (as mentioned above about fears).

For example, "I understand that your product has a good track record, but there's always a risk when trying out a new solution. What happens if it doesn't work out for us? Can you offer any assurances that we won't be left in a bad position?"

To overcome these objections, salespeople can use a variety of tactics and responses known as "overturns." (You'll want to customize these to fit your situation. Thank you, Captain Obvious!)

This discussion continues in the next chapter.

Chapter 48: Sales Objections and Overturns Continued...

Here are a few ways to prepare and respond, aka OVERTURN:

Overturns for Price: Offer a discount or special promotion or highlight the value or benefits of the product or service to justify the price.

(Note: I've provided additional overturns for the objection of price because it's one of the most common.)

Read this list and highlight the ones that resonate with you that you'd like to try on your next sales call.

"I understand that our price may seem high at first glance, but I can assure you that the value and quality of our product/service is worth the investment. Our product/service has X, Y, and Z features that make it stand out in the market, and it has helped other customers achieve X, Y, and Z benefits."

"We do have some options that may make our product/service more affordable for you. For example, we offer payment plans, bundle pricing, or loyalty discounts. Would you be interested in exploring these options?"

"I'm open to discussing the price further. Is there a specific budget you have in mind that you'd like to stay within? Maybe we can find a solution that works for both of us."

"I understand if the price is a concern for you. Thank you for considering our product/service. If you have any further questions or if you change your mind in the future, please don't hesitate to reach out."

Explain the value of your product or service and how it compares to competitors. Highlight any unique features or benefits that justify the price.

Offer a price comparison to show how your product or service compares in terms of value to similar products or services on the market.

Emphasize the long-term value of your product or service. If it is a durable or high-quality item that will last for a long time, it may be worth the higher price in the long run.

Be open to feedback and willing to listen to the customer's concerns. This can help you better understand their needs and find a solution that works for both parties.

Offer financing or payment options to make the product or service more accessible.

Negotiate with the customer to find a mutually beneficial solution. This could involve offering discounts or promotions, bundling products or services, or providing additional value in some other way.

If the customer is still unwilling to pay the full price, consider offering a lower-priced alternative or referral to a similar product or service. (See the other chapter on negotiating, don't just drop your price. Always sell on value, not price.)

Keep in mind, the price objection is almost always because the qualified prospect doesn't understand the value

Remember that not every customer will be willing to pay the full price, and it is okay to walk away from a deal if it is not a good fit for your business. Here are a few more overturns for the price objection:

"I know our price may seem a bit steep but think of it as an investment in your happiness. After all, you can't put a price on feeling fabulous."

"I understand that price is an important consideration for any purchase. But I want to make sure you understand the value of what you'll be getting. Our product/service is top-quality and offers a range of features and benefits that sets us apart from the competition. I believe that when you weigh the value of what we're offering against the price, you'll see that it's a worthwhile investment. Can I take a few minutes to walk you through some of the features and benefits that make us stand out?"

"I understand that our price may be higher than what you're used to paying, but I want to assure you that it reflects the level of quality and service we offer. We use the best materials, hire the most skilled professionals, and go above and beyond to ensure that our customers are completely satisfied. I believe that when you compare us to our competitors, you'll see that we offer the best value for your money. Can I tell you more about what sets us apart from the competition?"

"I understand that price is a factor for everyone, and I appreciate your concern. I want to assure you that we are competitively priced within our industry and that we offer a range of payment options to help make our product/service more accessible. I believe that when you consider the long-term value of what we're offering, you'll see that our price is well worth it. Can we explore some payment options that might work for you?"

Overturns for Lack of Need: Help the customer understand how the product or service will solve a problem or meet a specific need they may not be aware of.

"I understand that you may not think you need our product, but have you ever heard the saying 'I didn't know I needed it until I had it'? Trust me, you'll thank me later. May I continue..."

"I understand that you may not see an immediate need for our product, but I encourage you to think about the potential benefits it could bring in the future. Can I tell you more about how our product has helped other customers?"

"I understand that you may not think you need our product right now, but I encourage you to consider the long-term value it could bring. Can I tell you more about how our product can save you time, money, or hassle in the future?"

"I understand that you may not have a need for our product at the moment, but I encourage you to keep us in mind for the future. Our product has helped many other customers in ways they never expected. Can I tell you more about how our product could potentially benefit you in the future?"

Overturns for Lack of Time: Offer a time-saving solution or highlight the benefits of using the product or service in the long run.

"I know your schedule is jam-packed but think of how much time and stress our product will save you in the long run. Time is money, and this is a no-brainer."

"I get it, time is tight. But our product/service can actually save you time in the long run. Want to learn more?"

"Think long-term. Our product/service can save you time and hassle in the future. Interested in hearing more?"

"Our product/service simplifies your life and saves you time. Want to know how?"

Overturns for competitor Offerings: Differentiate your product or service from the competition and highlight its unique features and benefits.

"I understand that you're considering a competing product, but let me ask you this: do they have a team of highly trained unicorns working behind the scenes to make sure you get the best experience possible? I didn't think so."

"I understand that you're considering a competing product, but I encourage you to think about the level of support and customer service you'll receive. Our team is dedicated to providing the best experience possible for our customers, and we go above and beyond to ensure your satisfaction. Can I tell you more about the level of support and service you can expect from us?"

"I understand that you're considering a competing product, but I encourage you to think about the long-term value it will bring. Our product is designed to last and provide value over the long haul. By investing in a product that will stand the test of time, you'll save money in the long run and get a better return on your investment. Can I tell you more about the durability and reliability of our product?"

"I understand that you're considering a competing product, but I encourage you to think about the innovation and cutting-edge technology that our product offers. By choosing a product that is at the forefront of its industry, you'll have access to the latest and greatest solutions and features. Can I tell you more about the innovative features and technology that our product offers?"

Overturns for Risk: Offer a guarantee or trial period to help reduce the risk for the customer. It's essential that you identify their fears in advance, so you can preempt them during the sales presentation process.

"I understand that taking a risk can be scary, but let me put your mind at ease. We offer a 100% satisfaction guarantee, so if you're not completely thrilled with our product, we'll give you your money back. No questions asked."

"I understand that you may be hesitant to take a risk, but I encourage you to think about the potential benefits of our product. By investing in a solution that has helped many other customers achieve their goals, you could experience similar success. Can I tell you more about how our product has benefited other customers and how it could potentially benefit you?"

"I understand that you may be concerned about the risk of failure, but I assure you that our product has a proven track record of success. By choosing a product that has helped many other customers succeed, you can feel confident that it will work for you as well. Can I tell you more about the success our product has achieved for other customers?"

"I understand that you may be worried about conflict or other negative consequences, but I encourage you to think about the potential benefits of our product. By addressing the issues or challenges you're facing with a solution that has helped many other customers, you can move forward with confidence and achieve your goals. Can I tell you more about how our product has helped other customers overcome similar challenges?"

It's critically important to be prepared to handle objections and be able to effectively address them in advance of making a sales presentation.

Exercise:

Meet with your team and make a list of all the common objections that you get when selling your products and services.

This will vary greatly depending upon the types of products you sell and how complicated your sales process is as B2B sales are a lot different than B2C sales, but the objection categories are very similar. Practice. Practice. Practice. There's no such thing as perfection. Only improvement.

Good job! You still with me?

By understanding how to anticipate and address objections, you are now better equipped to handle difficult situations in the sales process. Remember to always listen carefully to your prospects and address their concerns with empathy and understanding.

By practicing and refining these approaches, you are building confidence in yourself and conveying it to your prospects, which ultimately will lead to increasing your sales.

I believe in you.

Chapter 49: Bouncing Back from Objections: Tips for Strengthening Your Resilience in Sales

We all know firsthand that objections are an inevitable part of selling. It can be tough to hear "no" or have your pitch challenged, but it's important to remember that objections are simply a chance for your potential customer to express their concerns and for you to address them.

Don't let rejection get you down — use it as an opportunity to showcase your skills, persistence, and resilience.

Remember, every objection is a chance to learn and grow, and with each one you overcome, you'll become even more confident and successful in your career.

Here are 6 ways to bounce back from objections:

1. **Don't take it personally:** As we mentioned earlier, objections aren't personal attacks. Remember that the customer is simply trying to make the best decision for themselves.

2. **Listen carefully:** It's important to listen carefully to the customer's objections and really understand what's behind them. This will help you tailor your response and address their concerns more effectively.

3. **Ask questions:** Asking clarifying questions can help you get to the root of the objection and understand the customer's needs and concerns better.

4. **Emphasize the value of your product or service:** It's important to remind the customer of the unique features and benefits of your product or service and how it can address their needs and solve their problems.

5. **Offer options or discounts:** If the customer is interested in your product or service but is concerned about the price, you could offer them options or discounts to make it more affordable.

6. **Respect the customer's decision:** If the customer decides not to purchase your product or service, it's important to respect their decision. Thank them for considering your offer and let them know

that you're always available if they have any further questions or if they change their mind.

Remember, resilience is all about bouncing back from challenges and setbacks. By understanding and accepting sales objections in a positive and proactive way, you'll be able to keep moving forward and make the most of every sales opportunity.

So, always keep in mind that every "no" is just one step closer to a "yes"!

Chapter 50: Win-Win Negotiations: Close More Deals and Build Stronger Relationships

As a salesperson, your ability to negotiate effectively can mean the difference between making a sale and coming up empty-handed.

But successful negotiation isn't just about getting what you want — it's about finding mutually beneficial solutions that leave both parties feeling satisfied.

In this chapter, we'll explore the skills and strategies you need to negotiate win-win deals that not only close more sales, but also help you build stronger, more productive relationships with your clients and customers.

Effective negotiation strategies and tactics can help you to achieve better outcomes in sales and other business negotiations. Here are some effective negotiation strategies and tactics.

Negotiation Strategies:

1. **Set clear goals and objectives:** As a salesperson for a local franchise business, it's important to have a clear understanding of what you want to achieve in the negotiation. This might include things like getting the best price for your products or services, securing a long-term contract, or establishing a new business relationship. To achieve these goals, it's important to communicate them clearly to the other party.

For example, you might say something like, "Our goal in this negotiation is to find a pricing structure that works for both of us, while also ensuring that we can provide the high-quality products and services that our customers have come to expect. What are your top priorities in this negotiation?"

2. **Research and prepare:** To negotiate effectively, it's important to have as much information as possible about the other party and the subject of the negotiation. This might include things like understanding their business (or personal) needs and goals, knowing their budget constraints, and being aware of any current market trends or competitive pressures. By doing your homework

beforehand, you'll be better equipped to present your case and find mutually beneficial solutions.

For example, if you're selling franchise opportunities for your local business, you might research the local market to understand the potential demand for your products or services or gather information about the competition to help position your offering as a strong choice.

3. **Establish rapport:** Building a positive relationship with the other party is key to successful negotiation. This means showing genuine interest in their needs and concerns and using open and honest communication.

For example, as a salesperson for a local franchise business, you might ask questions about the other party's business goals and objectives, listen actively to their concerns, and be transparent about your own needs and expectations. By establishing rapport and building trust, you'll be more likely to find common ground and reach a mutually beneficial agreement.

Negotiation Tactics:

1. **Use open-ended questions:** Use open-ended questions to gather more information and encourage the other party to share their perspective.

For example, you might ask, "Can you tell me more about your business and how you envision using our products or services?" or "What are your top concerns or priorities when it comes to this negotiation?"

Open-ended questions allow the other party to provide more detailed and informative responses, which can help you better understand their needs and position your offering in a more compelling way.

2. **Use positive body language:** Positive body language, such as making eye contact, smiling, and maintaining an open posture, can convey confidence and openness and help establish a more positive and productive negotiating environment.

For example, as a salesperson for a local franchise business, you might make eye contact with the other party and smile when discussing your offer or use open hand gestures to show that you're approachable and willing to listen.

3. **Make the first offer:** Making the first offer can give you an advantage by setting the initial terms of the negotiation. This allows you to establish a starting point and potentially shape the direction of the discussion.

For example, you might make an initial offer on price, terms, or other aspects of the deal.

By doing so, you can set the stage for further negotiation and give yourself a stronger bargaining position.

4. **Use deadlines:** Using deadlines can create a sense of urgency and encourage the other party to make a decision. This might involve setting a specific date by which the deal needs to be finalized or using other tactics like limited time offers or the availability of certain products or services.

For example, you might say something like, "We have a special offer available for the next week only, so if you're interested, I recommend making a decision sooner rather than later."

5. **Use multiple options:** Presenting multiple options to the other party, rather than just one, can give them more flexibility and increase the chances of reaching an agreement. This might involve offering different pricing structures, product or service packages, or terms of the deal.

For example, you might offer a range of options for the prospect to choose from, such as different levels of support, marketing materials, or training programs. By providing multiple options, you'll give the other party more choices and make it more likely that you'll be able to find a solution that meets their needs.

Remember, negotiation is about finding mutually beneficial solutions that leave both parties feeling satisfied.

By adopting this mindset (there's that word again) and applying the strategies we've discussed, you'll be well on your way to closing more deals and building stronger, more productive relationships with your clients and customers.

So go out there and negotiate with confidence, knowing that you have the skills and strategies you need to succeed.

Chapter 51: Sealing the Deal with Effective Closing Techniques

Effective **closing** techniques are the key to persuading potential customers to take the final step and make a purchase.

In this chapter, we'll explore a variety of techniques that you can use to seal the deal and turn leads into paying customers.

From building rapport to using powerful language, these strategies will help you increase your sales and grow your business, regardless of the franchise model. Again, adapt these to fit. Practice, practice, practice.

Authenticity an caring about the customer is critical to the success of closing techniques.

1. **The assumptive close:** This technique involves making an assumption that the customer is going to make a purchase, rather than asking them directly.

    For example, you might say,

    "I'll go ahead and process your order." or "I'll have your purchase delivered to your address."

    "Based on everything we've discussed today, it sounds like our product is a great fit for your needs. Can I go ahead and process your order now?"

    "It seems like our product is exactly what you're looking for. Shall we move forward with the purchase today?"

    "I'm confident that our product will exceed your expectations and solve your problem. Would you like to place your order now?"

2. **The trial close:** This technique involves asking a question that requires a positive response, in order to gauge the customer's level of interest.

For example, you might ask,

"Do you like the features of this product?" or "Would you like to see the color options?"

"Do you have any questions or concerns about our product before we move forward with the purchase?"

"What do you think about our product so far? Are you leaning towards making a purchase today?"

"Is there anything else you'd like to know about our product before you make a decision?"

3. **The alternative close:** This technique involves presenting the customer with a choice between two options, both of which lead to a sale.

    For example, you might say,

    "Would you like the red or the blue version of this product?" or "Would you prefer the monthly or annual payment plan?"

    "We have two different pricing options available for our product. Would you prefer the lower price with a shorter warranty, or the higher price with a longer warranty?"

    "We have two different delivery options available. Would you prefer to have the product delivered next week, or would you prefer to pick it up at our store?"

4. **The summation close:** This technique involves summarizing the main points of the sale and highlighting the benefits of the product or service. This can help to reinforce the value proposition and persuade the customer to make a purchase. Adapt, of course, to your specific offerings.

    For example, you might say,

    "To summarize, our homecare services include three visits per week from a licensed nurse, assistance with daily tasks like bathing and dressing, and access to 24/7 emergency support. Based on everything we've discussed, it sounds like our services would be a great fit for your loved one's needs. Are you ready to move forward with the purchase today?"

"Just to recap, our homecare services include a personalized care plan developed by our team of professionals, regular check-ins from a dedicated caregiver, and access to a wide range of resources and support. Based on what you've told me, it seems like our services would be the perfect solution for your needs. Shall we go ahead and finalize the purchase today?"

"As we've discussed, our homecare services include a range of flexible options to suit your loved one's needs, including hourly care, overnight care, and live-in care. We've also reviewed the pricing options and the benefits of our services. Based on everything we've talked about, do you feel comfortable moving forward with the purchase today?"

"To summarize, our homecare services include a comprehensive range of options to support your loved one's needs, including medical and non-medical care, transportation, and social support. We've also reviewed the pricing and payment options available. Based on everything we've discussed; it sounds like our services would be a great fit for your loved one. Are you ready to proceed with the purchase today?"

Closing deals is the name of the game. And by mastering a variety of effective closing techniques, such as the assumptive close, the trial close, and the summation close, you can take your sales skills to new heights.

These techniques, when refined and mastered, will help you persuade potential customers to take the final step and make a purchase, boosting your sales and growing your business.

So, don't be afraid to try new approaches and experiment with different techniques — with practice and persistence, you'll become a pro at sealing the deal. And who knows what amazing opportunities and rewards might be waiting for you on the other side of a successful close? So go out there and make it happen!

Chapter 52: Effective Follow-Up Strategies for Converting Interest into Action

Let's talk about the importance of effective follow-up sales strategies. We know that the sale doesn't end when you make the initial presentation or, as some old school sales professionals call it, the pitch.

Don't get distracted by verbiage. Call it what you'd like, but once you've sent or provided the proposal to your prospect, in fact, it's just the beginning. That's where the follow-up comes in.

Effective follow-up is key to building and maintaining relationships with potential and existing customers. It helps you stay top of mind, shows that you value their business, and ultimately leads to closing more deals. And in today's fast-paced world, it's more important than ever to stand out and make a lasting impression.

Side note: I reluctantly didn't include too much information about CRM systems because many of the franchise brands I work with already have an in-house system or preferred vendor.

Do you remember the chapter on TABOO TOPICS? Anyway, before we get to the follow-up strategies, it's important to consider your Client Relationship Management (CRM) system, marketing automation workflows, and how your other methods integrate into your marketing and sales processes.

If you've never used a CRM before, imagine you're a salesperson trying to juggle multiple customer accounts, each with their own unique needs and preferences. It can be a daunting task to keep track of everything — who you've contacted, what they're interested in, and where they are in the sales process. That's where a customer relationship management (CRM) system comes in.

Think of a CRM as a digital hub for all your customer interactions and information. It allows you to easily store and access everything you need to know about a customer, including communication history, sales pipeline, and important details about each account.

Plus, a CRM helps you to better understand your customers' needs and preferences, which can inform your sales strategy and help you close more deals. And with all of your data stored in one central location, it's easy to stay organized and on top of your sales game.

So, if you want to streamline your sales process, build stronger relationships with your customers, and make more informed, data-driven decisions, a CRM is a must-have tool in your sales tool kit. Now for the rest of the story…

There are many ways to approach follow-up, and it's important to find what works best for you and your customers.

Whether it's through email, phone calls, texting, in-person meetings, or snail mail, the key is to be consistent, professional, and personalized.

So, let's dive in and learn more ways to improve our follow-up skills:

1. **Personalize your follow-up:** Instead of sending a generic follow-up email, try personalizing it by addressing the customer by name and mentioning specific details from your previous conversation or proposal.

2. **Send a personalized video message:** This is my favorite. I love sending video messages because they engage more of the senses. Instead of sending a standard email or letter, consider recording a short video message that explains why your proposal is the best fit for the potential customer's needs. This can help you stand out and show that you're willing to go the extra mile.

3. **Offer a free trial or sample:** Consider offering a free trial, consultation, or sample to the potential customer. This can help them see the value of your offering firsthand and may increase the likelihood that they'll choose to do business with you

4. **Share customer testimonials or case studies:** You could send the customer a few testimonials or case studies from other satisfied customers to help build credibility and demonstrate the value of your service.

5. **Provide a special offer (LTO) or discount:** (Yes, really. This again.) You could offer the customer a special deal or discount to encourage them to move forward with your service. Covered this one a few times, huh.

6. **Follow up with a phone call:** Instead of just sending an email, you could try following up with a phone call to discuss the proposal in more detail and answer any questions the customer might have.

7. **Set a deadline:** You could set a deadline for the customer to make a decision, which might help them feel more motivated to act.

8. **Check in with them:** If the customer hasn't responded to your proposal, you could follow up with a simple email or phone call to check in and see if they have any questions or if there's anything else you can do to help them make a decision.

In this chapter, we explored the importance of developing effective follow-up skills in sales. We learned that the sale doesn't end when you make the initial pitch - in fact, it's just the beginning. That's where your follow-up skills and marketing automation comes in.

Effective follow-up is crucial to building and maintaining relationships with potential and existing customers. It helps you stay top of mind, show that you value their business, and ultimately close more deals.

By taking the time to nurture and cultivate relationships with your customers, you'll be able to close more deals and take your business to the next level. So, don't underestimate the power of follow-up — it's the key to unlocking your sales potential.

Chapter 53: The Power of Perseverance: Final Reflections on the Sales Process

Perseverance is a crucial quality to have when it comes to the sales process and overcoming obstacles.

Whether you're a top producer or new to selling, you can always get better. Here are a few additional ways to improve your sales skills:

1. **Seek out training and development opportunities:** Many companies offer sales training programs or allow their sales team to attend workshops or seminars to improve their skills. Look for opportunities to learn from experienced sales professionals and increase your knowledge of sales techniques and strategies.

2. **Practice, practice, practice:** (I've said that a few times throughout the book.) The more you practice your sales pitch and presentation skills, the more comfortable and confident you'll become. Consider role-playing with a colleague or mentor to get feedback and improve your delivery.

3. **Stay up to date on your industry and product knowledge:** Go to your brand's annual conference. Maybe I'll see you there if I'm selected as one of the keynote speakers, or maybe that's how you got this book, either way, go to them. Learn and network. It's important to have a deep understanding of your products or services, as well as your industry. Stay current on industry trends and news and be prepared to answer questions and address any concerns your customers may have.

4. **Build your network:** Building relationships with colleagues, customers, and industry professionals can be a valuable source of support and advice as you develop your sales skills. Attend industry events, join relevant online groups or associations, and seek out mentors who can provide guidance and advice.

5. **Monitor and track your progress:** This is another of the main purposes of a CRM. Keep track of your sales data and metrics to see how you're progressing over time. This can help you identify areas for improvement and set goals for yourself.

Final thoughts on improving your sales skills

With dedication and a willingness to constantly grow and learn, you can turn yourself into a top-performing salesperson and reach all of your ambitious goals.

By investing in your professional development and actively seeking out ways to improve, you'll set yourself up for success in the world of sales, in franchising or outside franchising.

So, don't be afraid to take on new challenges and push yourself to become the best version of yourself — with hard work, determination, and personal accountability you can achieve anything you want in business and life!

PART V — THE WINNING FORMULA: PLANNING, ACTION, AND ACCOUNTABILITY

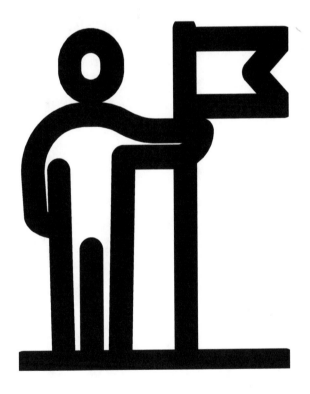

Chapter 54: Creating a Culture of Accountability

As you navigate the challenges and opportunities of owning and operating a franchise, I encourage continue to work on your personal accountability for your actions and inactions, your performance, and your results. This is essentially what PART I of *ACCELERATE* was focused on. It's worth an additional look.

Personal accountability is a crucial factor in achieving success in any business, and it involves accepting responsibility for your choices and the outcomes of those choices. And teaching your team about accountability and consequences too.

When we take personal accountability for our work, we are empowered to make positive changes and to take ownership of our tasks and responsibilities. This leads to improved performance and results, as well as increased customer satisfaction and trust within our organizations.

The Buck Stops Here: Building a Culture of Accountability in Your Business

Creating a culture of accountability is essential for building trust and driving results in your business. It involves setting clear expectations for personal responsibility, leading by example, and providing the necessary resources and support.

This results in a positive work environment that inspires teamwork and innovation, leading to greater success. Hold yourself and your team accountable for their actions and decisions to build a culture of trust and collaboration.

I believe that you have the potential to achieve great success as a franchise owner or franchisee. But it won't happen without taking personal accountability.

So, I encourage you to embrace this idea and to take ownership of your actions and their outcomes. This will not only lead to improved performance and results, but it will also help you to build confidence, trust, and a sense of accomplishment.

Remember to:

- **Set clear goals:** Identify what you want to achieve and create specific, measurable, achievable, relevant, and time-bound (SMART) goals.

- **Take ownership of your tasks and responsibilities:** Be proactive in completing your work and finding solutions to problems that arise.

- **Communicate openly and honestly:** Be transparent with your team and stakeholders about your progress and any challenges you may face.

- **Seek feedback:** Ask for feedback from your team, supervisor, or mentor to identify areas for improvement and develop a plan to address them.

- **Learn from your mistakes:** Don't let setbacks or failures discourage you. Instead, use them as opportunities to learn and grow.

- **Take initiative:** Don't wait for someone else to tell you what to do. Take initiative and be proactive in finding ways to contribute and make a difference.

Regardless of your role, accountability starts with you, the reader...

Be accountable for your actions: Accept responsibility for your choices and the outcomes of those choices. Don't make excuses or shift blame to others. You have the power to create the success you desire as a franchise owner, leader, manager, or frontline staff person.

Continue to take personal accountability for your actions and watch as your success unfolds.

Chapter 55: Creating Your Massive Action Plan (MAP)

Welcome to one of the final steps in the journey to achieve your goals — creating your massive action plan (MAP).

A massive action plan is a road map that outlines the specific steps you need to take to achieve your goals. It helps you stay focused and motivated, and ensures that you are taking consistent, measurable action towards your desired outcomes.

Please use the space on the next few pages to gain clarity on your top priorities and action items as a result of reading this book.

Today's Date _____

My Name _____

My Top 3 Business Improvement Goals are:

Why I Will Follow Through:

Top 10 Action Steps I'll Get Done

1. _____

2. _____

3. _____

4. _____

5. _____

6. _____

7. _____

8. _____

9. _____

10. _____

5 Keys to Starting This Week!

1. _____

2. _____

3. _____

4. _____

5. _____

10 Other Things I Will Get Done Within 90 Days!

1. _____

2. _____

3. _____

4. _____

5. _____

6. _____

7. _____

8. _____

9. _____

10. _____

NOTES:

Chapter 56: Now the Fun Stuff Begins...

Congratulations. You're just about to complete this book. But your journey is only beginning.

It's going to be a journey of challenge, adventure, and growth. By now you are hopefully feeling inspired and empowered to take your marketing efforts on a continuing progression toward higher success.

Don't forget to celebrate your successes along the way. Every small victory is a step closer to achieving your goals.

Remember to key on three things...

First, local marketing is all about building connections with your community and understanding the needs and wants of your target audience. By creating a strong local presence and delivering targeted, relevant content, you can effectively reach and engage your customers.

Second, every franchise model and local business is unique and what works for one location or territory may not work for another. It's important to test different strategies and tactics and see what resonates with your audience and track your KPIs. Don't be afraid to get creative and think outside the box, but within the box of franchise guidelines and best practices. *My last disclaimer.*

Third, it's crucial to stay up to date on the latest trends and technologies in local marketing. A great way to do that is by subscribing to FORDIFY.TV and the FORDIFY LIVE Podcast.

You'll discover timely and topical case studies from franchise executives and guest experts, as we dig deep on the topics of franchising success, marketing, sales, Customer Experience (CX), and Employee Experience (EX). By staying on top of trends, and what's working and what's not working — you can ensure that your business acceleration efforts are effective and relevant.

To truly accelerate your business growth, it's essential to take consistent, strategic action towards your goals and always be open to learning and growing.

You have the tools and knowledge you need to reach the next level, so don't hold back – it's time to put them into action! Believe in yourself and your abilities, and don't be afraid to take calculated risks.

Go out there and make a positive impact in your community. I believe in your ability to achieve greatness.

Because I believe in you!

Recommended Resources

Accelerating Revenue Growth Training Workshops

Reach your goals even faster! Let us design a customized training workshop or virtual training series specifically designed to help you and your team gain more profound knowledge and implementation of the concepts, strategies, and doable tactics to address your top challenges. The process starts with a confidential discovery call to discuss your specific outcomes, roles, and goals.

Keynote Presentations and Virtual Training Solutions for B2B & B2C Franchise Brands.

Fired Up is Nice... But Fueled Up is Better!

ELEVATE PERFORMANCE | ACCELERATE GROWTH | GENERATE HIGHER PROFITS

What makes Ford Saeks the top-choice speaker for franchises brands such as Subway®, Papa Murphy's, MTY Group, Comfort Keepers®, Senior Helpers®, Orangetheory Fitness®, Precision Door, Wine & Design, Learning Express Toys, Lawn Doctor, Gold's Gym, Image360, Alliance Franchise Brands, the International Franchise Association (IFA), and many others?

Ford Saeks has a diverse range of experience in multiple industries from retail, QSR, fast-casual, full-service dining, and residential and commercial services. Ford has experience working with emerging franchise brands with under 100 units up to large global brands with over 20,000 franchise locations.

Before planning his presentation, he works closely with you and your planning committee to capture your specific outcomes. Then he mystery shops a few locations of your choice, usually a few heroes and underperformers, to make sure the presentation is timely, topical, and relevant. He also becomes a third-party endorsement for key initiatives that you may want him to reinforce to your franchisees. Many brands also have Ford interview their franchise advisory committee leadership for their insights too.

Ford uses a fun, interactive style to engage audiences with his valuable small business wisdom. Franchisees leave Ford's live and virtual sessions with tons of ideas and ready-to-implement action steps IN ALIGNMENT WITH YOUR BRAND to produce immediate results. His takeaways are perfect for single unit and multi-unit franchise owners.

5 Reasons Why You Need a Franchise Keynote Speaker with Experience

When you're planning an event for your franchisees, it's essential to choose the right keynote speaker that doesn't put your event at risk. An experienced franchise keynote speaker can help your owners understand the importance of following your systems and how to expand their local brand awareness.

Ford understands franchising. The franchisor wants their franchisees to follow their systems and take personal accountability for their local marketing and success.

He provides valuable insights on growing a franchise business.

His presentations are engaging and relevant to address today's top challenges.

Ford has helped thousands of franchisees increase performance, improve the customer experience, and increase sales.

As the opening keynote speaker, he will kick off your conference with a bang. As the closing keynote speaker, he will ensure your Zees leave with a prioritized massive action plan.

About the Author

The Business Growth Expert

Ford Saeks is more than a hall of fame keynote speaker, he's a research-based thought leader. An engine. An expert. An idea man and marketing machine. He helps businesses not by talking at them about success, but by talking them through the steps to get there.

Ford started his first business at 15 years old and has been succeeding ever since. He has redefined the formula for business growth. His efforts have helped companies generate more than $1 billion in sales worldwide.

From start-ups to Fortune 500s, Saeks is widely recognized as a business growth expert. With over 30 years of experience (ranging from retail to wholesale), he has founded more than ten companies, authored six books, secured three U.S. patents, and earned numerous industry awards.

Give us a call at 1-800-946-7804 or 316-844-0245
or online at www.FranchiseTrainingSolutions.com

Watch Ford's Keynote Speaker Trailer >>

Skyrocket Results

In his popular keynotes or in his private consultations, Ford helps businesses find a way forward. That means first identifying what it is that is holding them back. There is a gap between where they want to be and where they are now.

Once business owners are clear on their gap and put the right mindset, strategies, and tactics into place, the results are extraordinary. They see radical growth in the business.

Take A Page Out of Ford's Book(s)

Ford Saeks is an author with your success in mind. His books offer expert advice, action steps, and other useful takeaways for the motivated entrepreneur, business owner, CEO, marketing professional, and manager.

SUPERPOWER! A Superhero's Guide to Leadership, Business, and Life makes a great addition to your success library

Mover, Shaker, Rainmaker

Tenacity and innovation are what fuel this revenue-generating powerhouse. From grassroots to Google, Ford provides his clients with fresh perspectives and doable tactics to resolve marketing, operations, and growth challenges.

As President and CEO of Prime Concepts Group, Inc., a creative marketing agency, Ford specializes in helping businesses attract loyal and repeat buyers, monetize social media, and ignite creativity. Visit www.PrimeConcepts.com.

Connect with Ford Saeks Online

WATCH: Visit www.Fordify.TV and subscribe to his YouTube Channel to watch upcoming video episodes on Business Success, Marketing & Sales, Customer Experience, and more…

LISTEN: Subscribe to the Accelerating Business Growth PODCAST hosted by Ford Saeks at: www.ProfitRichResults.com/podcast

- Apple
- Spotify
- Anchor
- and other platforms

SHARE: www.FranchiseTrainingSolutions.com

DISCOVER: www.ProfitRichResults.com

CREATIVE AGENCY: www.PrimeConcepts.com

LINKEDIN: www.LinkedIn.com/in/fordsaeks

TWITTER: www.Twitter.com/prime_concepts

FACEBOOK: www.Facebook.com/profitrichresults

INSTAGRAM: www.Instagram.com/fordsaeks

TIKTOK: www.tiktok.com/@fordsaeks

Yes, This is the last page and final easter egg. Get a copy of ACCELERATE for everyone on your team. It sure be great if you'd leave me an Amazon review, (you know 5-stars) along with positive comments, so more people can find and benefit from this book.

Thanks for joining me on this journey. Keep in Touch.

CPSIA information can be obtained
at www.ICGtesting.com
Printed in the USA
BVHW050150090223
658191BV00013B/442/J